PORSCHE

ICONIC CARS

CAR AND DRIVER

filipacchi
publishing

Contents

Introduction 6

Porsche 1600 Speedster *(June 1956)* 8

Porsche 1600 Normal Coupe *(May 1958)* 14

Porsche 911 S *(January 1967)* 19

Porsche Speedster *(September 1967)* 24

Porsche 914 - 914/6 *(December 1969)* 32

Porsche Turbo Carrera *(December 1975)* 34

Porsche 912 E *(December 1975)* 38

Porsche 928 and 930 *(April 1978)* 41

Porsche 944 *(May 1982)* 50

James Dean's Spyder *(October 1985)* 57

Porsche 959 *(November 1987)* 64

Porsche Boxster *(November 1996)* 68

Porsche Boxster vs. Mercedes-Benz SLK vs. BMW Z3 2.8 *(April 1997)* 72

Porsche Cayenne Turbo *(August 2003)* 80

Porsche Carrera GT *(December 2003)* 85

Porsche 911 Carrera S *(November 2004)* 88

Porsche 911 Carrera vs. Chevrolet Corvette Z51 *(December 2004)* 92

Porsche Cayman S *(July 2005)* 100

Porsche Cayman S vs. Lotus Exige *(March 2006)* 102

10 Best Cars: Porsche Boxster and Cayman *(January 2009)* 108

Porsche Panamera *(May 2009)* 112

Porsche 911 Turbo *(January 2010)* 116

Porsche 911 Turbo vs. Chevrolet Corvette ZR1 *(April 2010)* 120

Introduction

For many enthusiasts, the name Porsche is enough to define the modern sports car.

Essential, emotional, and exotic, Porsche and its vehicles may be attainable only for a small portion of the driving public, but they're known instantly by millions more— for their iconic styling as much as their inescapable performance.

And for true aficionados, Porsche is known for engineering. Founded before World War II by its namesake, Ferdinand Porsche, the company turned the Volkswagen Beetle from concept into automotive history—and then set out after the war on a quest to build highly precise, high-performance sports cars, one painstakingly perfected piece at a time.

In the decades since, Porsche has built, sold, and raced some of the finest vehicles ever known. It's broadened and buffed its portfolio beyond sports cars to include sedans and sport-utility vehicles. And while it's careened from corporate drama to corporate drama—including this decade's aborted takeover of Volkswagen—it's remained true to its mission, even while it's stretched the notion of what makes a vehicle a true Porsche.

Porsche came into being in 1931, and yet its status as an enthusiast icon would take another generation to ripen. Founded by Professor Porsche with his son-in-law, Anton Piech, the company was charged with developing the idea of a people's car into a practical, mass-market vehicle. The result: the Volkswagen Beetle, which would go on to become the top-selling vehicle of all time, and a constant player in the history of Porsche through the 1960s.

The company's roots in the design of the original Beetle might have steered it into a mainstream, mass-market role in the car universe. Porsche, the engineer, would see his son Ferry turn the VW basics into a new sportscar, which would become the 356. One of the first vehicles produced in Germany after the war, the 356 would only gradually evolve away from the Beetle basics, but it gave the fledgling carmaker its early reputation for exciting handling. Before long, Porsche had begun selling cars in America, and one very famous American owner lent the car and the brand some of his own danger-seeking flair— even before he died behind the wheel of his 550 Spyder,

James Dean helped launch Porsche into the sports-car stratosphere.

In the early 1960s, Porsche started over. Knowing the shortcomings of its existing sports cars, it sketched out a new vehicle with the engine still hung off the rear, but with every other detail, every other part made new. The powerplant grew to six cylinders, arranged in horizontally opposed banks. The new coupe body tapered into an effortlessly elegant teardrop. The result: the instant classic, the Porsche 911, a model that endures today with those basic elements in place, if dramatically stretched, pushed and pressed to their limits.

The 911 has survived precisely because of its truth to its purpose. Throughout the 1960s, and into the 1970s, engineers kept refining its tricky handling, while upping the output of its flat-six "boxer" engine to stunning levels. Various S and SC models came and went, along with Cabriolet and Targa body styles; the addition of the "Type 930" 911 Turbo threw down a gauntlet to the world's best drivers who found its devilish handling even beyond their talents.

By the 1980s, the 911 had survived multiple attempts on its corporate life, and instead of growing weary and resolute, it got tougher—with still more power, and with a new all-wheel-drive system pioneered in the limited-edition 959 supercar. Essentially all-new for only the second time in 1989, the 911 would go on to reiterate itself three more times, with each of five generations bearing the same sloping tail and fearsome performance of the originals— save a four-cylinder misstep like the 912, or two.

In its modern era, the 911 is with few peers. Today's 911 Turbo spins out nearly 500 horsepower from half the displacement of a Corvette V-8. With all-wheel drive and all types of electronic traction and stability aids, the 911 also handles with the safety of a luxury sedan. And still, it's time for renewal—with a new 911 due sometime in 2012.

The flat-six-powered 911 has endured, even as Porsche spun off new model lines to complement its icon. Not each has been a resounding success, but Porsche's track record has gotten notably stronger in the past two decades, after some serious off-track ventures in the 1970s and 1980s.

While the 911 flourished, Porsche hunted in the 1970s for a less expensive vehicle—one a little more in tune with its roots. Twice Porsche failed to step in the right direction. The first attempt at a low-cost Porsche bred the 914, a mid-engine targa-topped two-seater that had been planned as a Volkswagen roadster in four-cylinder form, and a Porsche when fitted with six cylinders. It arrived in 1970 wearing only Porsche badges—and it wasn't until 1974 that the hot-selling, but slow-accelerating 914 began to earn some of its street cred.

On the heels of the 914, Porsche began development work for VW on a new sportscar. When the two-door coupe was axed before it went on sale, Porsche decided to acquire rights to sell the vehicle and dubbed it the 924. With Porsche DNA buried under lackluster Audi drivetrains, the 924 nonetheless won praise for its handling, and held a place in its niche.

Porsche simultaneously delivered the hefty, V-8-powered 928 coupe. The grand tourer seeded the ground for an eventual retirement of the classic 911, but the 928's luxury proved less popular than the classic 911's purity, and sales were slow—ironic since the 928 was among the fastest vehicles in the world, in its heyday. It was retired in the mid-1990s.

The only new Porsche from this era to succeed on a level anything close to the 911, was the dazzling 944. Based on the same front-engine, rear-drive principle as the 924, the 944's swollen fenders, Porsche-engineered powertrains and perfectly balanced handling forever changed the idea of what constituted a Porsche. As it added Turbo, Cabriolet and S variants over its nine-year history, the 944 did what all the other recent new Porsches could not—it paved the way for a new generation of striking, strong-selling, non-911 Porsches.

In the early 1990s, Porsche's financial condition was delicate. On the edge of insolvency and saddled with high costs, Porsche turned to Toyota for new ways of building its vehicles more efficiently, and more effectively. At the same time, it turned inward for inspiration and looked to the Spyders and 356s of the past as it planned a new entry-level sports car.

The result would be the Boxster, a stunning success in all ways, from engineering to sales. The Boxster, and its later Cayman coupe companion, delivered to Porsche the same essence that the 911 always had. Exceptional handling, a flat-six engine hammering away behind the driver's ears, and a sleek body only a Xerox or two removed from the 550 Spyder reinvigorated the interest in Porsche from anyone unable, or uninterested, in owning a 911. The lessons learned from Toyota turned the Boxster and the 911 into cash machines, too—and by the end of the century, Porsche was the industry's most profitable brand.

Those profits allowed Porsche the luxury of planning two entirely new vehicle lines in one decade. The first, the mud-worthy Cayenne sport-utility vehicle, arrived to much controversy in 2003, with followers failing to make a dent in its performance or its ability—but unable at first to connect the vehicle with the nameplate in a logical way. The introduction of a Cayenne Turbo, quick enough to pace the base 911, did much to fill in the credibility gap.

Then in 2010, Porsche fulfilled the stillborn promise of a late-1980s sedan concept, then dubbed the 989. The thrilling Panamera sedan executed the promise of a truly adult-sized four-seat sports car, with an extra pair of doors added for convenience. With only a few notices for its ungainly rear end, the staggeringly fast and nimble Panamera won over the faithful and the doubters at the first turn of its steering wheel. It did more. The Panamera proved for once and for all that, no matter which vehicle wore its badges, the name "Porsche" always came first.

As Porsche transformed itself into a sports-car legend, automotive enthusiasts in America saw it unfold from the driver's seat. In 1955, Sports Car Illustrated hit newsstands, reporting on European racing series and auto maintenance. In short order, the magazine turned its focus to new car reviews and to car culture—and in 1961, it christened its new mission under a new name, *Car and Driver*.

In Porsche's modern era, *Car and Driver* has been a faithful chronicler. We've covered everything from the first road tests of the newest vehicles to wear the Stuttgart stamp of approval to classic feature stories that dropped an unearthly 935 race car into the middle of a Kansas high-school reunion and top-speed testing of the experimental 959.

Car and Driver witnessed—and played a role in—the Porsche experience. For the first time, the magazine's best Porsche stories have been brought together in a timeline of 0-to-60-mph times and top speeds, with unforgettable photos from the distant and recent past. To give you the essential flavor of the marque's history over time, and to show the evolution of *Car and Driver* as well, our original stories have been reproduced as they were published.

Buckle up, and hit reverse with us as we power through a remarkable six decades of Porsche history as we've seen it—through the fifth wheels and camera lenses of *Car and Driver*.

SCI
tests the porsche
speedster 1600

Photos by Griff Borgeson

Rear engine design of Porsche keeps the Stuttgart machine clean and uncluttered in front. Bumper is protected by inserted rubber strip.

"... one of the most significant technical accomplishments of our time."

T HE NEW Porsche 1600 is one of the world's truly fine cars. Every hour you spend with it adds to your appreciation of the excellence of its design, workmanship, and performance. It's a supremely good machine in traffic or on the open highway and a world-beater on winding roads. It makes you hunger for a handy Alp to slide up and down all day. As a precision instrument for maintaining high average speeds regardless of terrain, it's a revelation.

At no increase in price over its 1500 cc predecessor, the 1600 offers six percent increases in horsepower and displacement and a five percent increase in torque. Calculations based on the car's pulling power and tractive resistance indicate that the actual output of the 1582 cc, 96.5 cubic inch engine is more, not less, than the factory-advertised 70 bhp figure. The Speedster, as the roadster model is called, lists at $2995 at U. S. port of entry and can be driven away for about $3200 after all fees and compulsory options have been cared for. You don't get much iron as such for your money but you do get an engineering masterpiece in the full, literal sense of the term.

Sparewheel, fuel tank, jack, tools, and space for small articles of luggage ride up forward of the driver. Stone guards protect headlamps from flying road debris.

Porsche's tail slides toward outside of bend on standard test curve. This curve is not on a slope despite optical illusion, road is dead level. Car's driftability helps it achieve high average speeds.

Brakes of early Porsches fell short of perfection until 1952 when the larger bimetal drum with two-leading shoes was made standard for all production cars. The larger drum, shown here, makes stopping distances short without locking the wheels.

Even though this is a country in which the fact or illusion of size is often a criterion of quality, enough Americans dig the Porsche right now so that, if not another order were placed, the factory could continue to operate at full tilt for at least a couple of years. The cars are *very* difficult to come by. For example, the last shipment for the Southwest consisted of ten 1600's to be doled out among 38 howling dealers. I managed to obtain a test car only by the grace of the deity and film producer Manny Post, whose passion for Porsches caused him to add Europa Motors of North Hollywood to his properties. Mr. Post handed me the keys to his personal, spanking new Speedster and said, "Don't let the low milage inhibit you. Just get the lube oil warm, then go ahead and stand on it." His instructions were obeyed to the letter and with profoundly educational results.

In a road test last month I mentioned that I am not an exponent of the controlled slide. Now, thanks to living with the Porsche for a few days, I am.

I don't like to push my driving prejudices at others but it's necessary here to illustrate the point. In a car with a mushy, tentative road-bite I drive with caution born of doubt. In a car with a tenacious, glued feel I'm so grateful for the being-on-rails sensation that I have no desire to exchange it for a technique of skidding that would only serve a purpose in competition. And then along comes the Porsche.

Its engine, of course, is mounted at the rear, aft of the pendulum-type rear axle. Our test car, with the fuel tank about three-quarters full, weighed 1680 lbs. and almost 58 percent of this bore on the rear wheels. The springing is typically Porsche, by laminated transverse torsion bars acting through trailing links at the front and solid, adjustable transverse bars at the rear acting through trailing arms. The unorthodox weight distribution and suspension give the car handling qualities that are rather unique. At slow speeds it handles quite normally in turns, and the feel is on the moderately "glued" side. Then, at only slightly higher speed, its character changes entirely. In place of a four-square chassis bite on the road you have the rear end of the car slipping toward the outside of the curve.

Most of us have an instinctive aversion to this sensation which, in the average car, means you've lost it. When it happens to you in a Porsche for the first time you're more than likely to be startled if not plainly scared. This rear-end slip is *not* like that of a "glued" chassis when it hits a patch of dirt —biting firmly, then sideslipping for a split second, then snapping into the rails again. The Porsche does not break away suddenly. It drifts from inside to outside in a gentle, casual way. The sensation is very much like cornering on half-inflated tires.

Is this bad? Only if you believe it is. Is it good? Emphati-

In moderate turns, the Speedster is slipped through under power all the way, directing the car by a combination of rear-wheel or four-wheel slip and throttle.

cally yes, if you accept and understand it. You can corner a Porsche in a sedate and conventional manner if you choose. Just as easily, you can wag its tail and get through short, tight-radius turns with amazing nimbleness and speed. In more open curves you can drift all four wheels and the smooth transition from bite to slip is almost imperceptible.

The slip effect is as though the car were on a pivot at the front end. You pop the Porsche into a tight turn, deliberately flip the rear end outward so that the car is perfectly aimed to leave the turn, then head for the straight under full acceleration. In turns that are not too tight you can steam through under power all the way, directing the car by a combination of steering wheel, rear-wheel or four-wheel slip, and throttle. Thanks to these characteristics and a set of magnificent brakes the Porsche is hilariously controllable and agile.

PERFORMANCE
PORSCHE 1600 SPEEDSTER

TOP SPEED
(At sea level, with 1.5 mile approaches to ¼-mile timing traps.)
Two-way average ......97.3 mph
Fastest one-way run ..98.1 mph

ACCELERATION
From zero to:
20 mph	2.1 secs.
30	4.6
40	7.1
50	9.5
60	13.3
70	16.6
80	20.7
Standing ¼ mile	18.8
Standing mile	49.6 (72.5 mph avg)

SPEEDS IN GEARS
Recommended max.:
First	15 mph
Second	49
Third	71

SPEEDOMETER CORRECTION
20 mph indicated	19 mph actual
30	27
40	37
50	46
60	56
70	66
80	75
90	84

FUEL CONSUMPTION
Hard test driving, actual ....18.9 mpg
Moderate cruising, estimated ....28 - 30 mpg

SPECIFICATIONS

POWER UNIT
Type ....Opposed four, air cooled
Valve arrangement ....Vee-inclined, pushrod operated
Idle speed ....900 rpm
Maximum bhp ....70 bhp @ 4500 rpm
Maximum torque ......82 lb. ft. @ 2700 rpm
Piston displacement..96.5 cu. ins./1582 cc.
Bore and stroke ....3.25 x 2.91 ins./82.5 x 74 mm
Stroke-bore ratio ....0.89 to one
Compression ratio ....7.5 to one

DRIVE TRAIN
Transmission ratios....
I —	3.18 - 1
II —	1.76 - 1
III —	1.13 - 1
IV —	0.815 - 1

CHASSIS
Suspension, front ......Porsche trailing links and transverse laminated torsion bars
Suspension, rear ....Swinging half-axles, adjustable transverse torsion bars, trailing arms
Shock absorbers ....Tubular double-acting
Steering wheel turns..2¼, lock to lock
Turning diameter ....33 feet
Brakes ....Two leading shoe front hydraulics; ribbed light alloy drums, cast iron liners
Brake lining area ......124 sq. ins.
Wheel studs ....5½-in. studs; 8 in. circle diameter
Tire size ....5.00 x 16
Rim width (outside) ..4.6 ins
Wheelbase ....83 ins.
Tread ....50.8 ins. F./49.2 ins. R.

Profile view of Porsche speedster with top up. It can be erected in half a minute by one man.

Frame of the Porsche is constructed of pressed steel welded in box section form. Longitudinal members are built up as large thin-walled sections which provide maximum resistance under moments of stress. Tunnel in middle of frame is passage for gear shift rods, and other control cables.

Tool kit. TOP: Tire gauge; rubber spark plug sheath; and spark plug. CENTER: Cutting pliers; stubby screwdriver; screwdriver; four metric-sized wrenches; generator pulley wrench; lug wrench; and spark plug wrench. Extra fan belt is strapped to tool kit case.

GENERAL
Length	155 ins.
Width	65 ins.
Height	51 ins.
Weight, test car	1680 lbs.
Weight distribution F/R	42.5/57.5

RATING FACTORS
Bhp per cu. in.	.72
Bhp per sq. in. piston area	2.11
Pounds per bhp, test car	24.0
Piston speed @ 60 mph	1518 ft. per min.
Piston speed @ max. bhp	2185 ft. per min.
Brake lining area per ton, test car	148 sq. ins.

Drifting this ultra-light car seems to have no undue effect on tire wear. Charging down a steep mountain road containing 63 hairpin switchbacks produced the impression that the 1600 spent all its time on the tires' sidewalls. But at the bottom I got out and checked the German Dunlops and found that the shoulder where tread joins sidewall was as sharp as when new. Incidentally, marks were made on the rims and sidewalls at the beginning of the road test. In spite of much heavy acceleration and braking, there was *no* slippage of the tires on the rims.

It's clear that the Porsche's delightful "driftability," which helps it to achieve high average speeds, impressed me as the car's most spectacular feature. But it's a distinguished car in many other ways.

In spite of its light weight the 1600 is rock-solid and stable at all speeds. There is scarcely any perceptible difference in sensation inside the car between speeds of 20 and 80 mph. Above that, our test machine's suspension became slightly harsh, possibly because it was too new for lubricant to have fully penetrated the leaves of the laminated front torsion bars. In common with the ride of many continental cars, the 1600's is slightly firm on a good road surface and scarcely different on the very worst surface.

The steering, like most of the Porsche's other organs, is superlative; the *right now* kind—quick, light, positive, and completely devoid of play. It is very sensitive to tire pressures. When I received the test car it was carrying "town" tire pressures of 20 lbs. front and 26 lbs. rear. While this

(Continued on page 56)

Porsche Speedster

(Continued from page 17)

gave an extremely comfortable ride, although too soft for optimum cornering, it was not until pressures had been raised to 28 front and 32 rear that the full precision of the steering could be enjoyed. It's not the sort that seems to anticipate your commands, it just translates them into instantaneous movement. It contributes to the solid, stolid feel of the whole car. It has a few ounces of resistance to any change in direction which renders the system steady, but effortless to operate. I drove as far as a half-mile at a stretch with my hands away from the fine-feeling, 15½ inch wheel. The car, travelling at 55 mph, held a perfectly straight line.

The 1600's brakes are as good as its steering. The brakes of early Porsches fell considerably short of perfection until 1952, when the big, bimetal-drum, two leading-shoe hydraulics used on the Liege-Rome-Liege rally winners were made standard for all production Porsches. These brakes have as much authority at 100 mph as they do at ten. Stopping distances are laughably short *without* locking the wheels, without leaving skid marks. These powerful stops scarcely pitch the passengers at all and fade failed to show during deliberate, demanding downhill tests.

The Porsche's four-speed all-synchro transmission with overtop fourth is another factor in determining this car's unique personality. On up-shifts the smooth, silent, butter-slicing engagement of gears is uncanny, positively spellbinding. On down-shifts it's the same, providing speed limits are not exceeded. These limits are 62 mph for shifting into third, 37 for second and 12 for first. However, equally smooth down-shifts can be made from higher speeds by use of the simplest crash box double-kick technique. This gearbox design was created originally for the stillborn Cisitalia Formula I car and has since been used on Ferrari and Maserati grand prix machines. Enough said.

On the negative side for a change, the floor-shift lever is long and springy and the shifting linkage has a spongy feel. The lever's travel is excessive and getting it into reverse frequently degenerates into a stubborn struggle between drive and mechanism. Even when reverse (not synchromesh, of course) can be engaged readily, merely overcoming the spring-loaded safety re-

quires far too much muscle power. The clutch takes hold softly and smoothly but its pedal travel also is undesirably long.

Some previous Porsche models have been guilty of excessive engine noise even when new, but this charge cannot be brought against the new 1600. With its 900 rpm idle it emits a pleasant, low-level buzz when standing still. In motion, those riding in the car can hardly hear the engine at all. A very faint, pleasant chirp, probably in the venturis of the twin Solex carbs, is the most pronounced sound, and it is only apparent when manifold vacuum drops. The exhaust note is an impeccable purr. The designers know their bite is good; they can do without an exhibitionistic bark.

Although the 1600 engine's published torque curve is fairly flat and high from 2000 to 4000 rpm, it struggles against its harness for a long moment in getting away from a dead stop. This is in spite of the fact that first gear is abnormally low. Once the engine starts winding in this gear the rev counter is redlined in less than two seconds, calling for a lot of alertness on the part of the driver who wants to get the most out of every shift. It's much better for the engine not to wind it too tight in first but to get into second as soon as the car is rolling nicely, say at about 3000 rpm. The red "pie slice" on the rev counter starts at 4500.

Third gear in the 1600 is tremendously handy, offering gutty acceleration from about 25 to 70 mph. The less than one-to-one fourth is surprising for its pulling power. It's perfectly adequate for tooling along in traffic all day. The town driver in a hurry can stay in the very flexible third; he'll have no trouble in staying with or leaving the horsepower leviathans.

One of the most salient of the 1600's features is its solid, built to last and last feel. Its body is this way. When you close the light doors they seat with a *chunk* that translates as quality. On one occasion I drove about ten miles before discovering that one door was on the half-latched position — it had not rattled once.

There were no squeaks or rattles at all in the test car's body and everything worked perfectly and smoothly — doors, hood, engine cover and, above all, the convertible top. This is a device that

one person can raise or fold in half a minute and with complete ease. Being simple, perfect, and well finished it is in harmony with the rest of the car.

Its paint is like porcelain. The upholstery is of very good quality. The small, curved windshield is beautifully and substantially mounted and is without visual distortion. The method of mounting the rear view mirror makes it possible for a driver of any height to make the adjustment that is exactly right for him. The bucket seats have ventilated backs and a wide range of fore and aft adjustment. Heat from the air-cooled engine supplies a built-in heating and demisting system in the passenger compartment. For a car of its very modest dimensions luggage space behind the seats is good and of course there is more useful space under the hood. A couple of suitcases or overnight bags can be carried in the Speedster with no strain. The only area in which there's an aching need for more space is that where the occupants' feet must repose. It's narrow, and it enforces a position that can be tiring on a long run.

The spare tire and wheel are stowed under the hood, at the front of the car. Also in that space are the fuel tank (1.5 gallon reserve), a dip stick, a jack built to outlast ten cars, and a tool kit. This contains a set of fine metric endwrenches, a special spark plug wrench (without which you're likely to be grounded), one of the world's best lugnut wrenches, a fine dial-type tire pressure gauge and a number of other tools. Also in the kit are spare drive belts, a spark plug and, just in case, an extra lug nut. Such a set in this country would cost about $25, yet it comes with the **Porsche** and is *not* an extra.

When our test was complete, Mr. Post's personal 1600 still had less than 500 miles on its speedometer. This optimistic instrument had been pushed to indicate almost 110 mph at an actual clocked speed of 98 mph. If the saying is true that if you want a car to be fast you should break it in fast, this should be a rapid car indeed. One thing for certain is that in another 1000 miles it will be capable of breaking an honest 100 mph and its acceleration times will be even better. #

SCI ROAD TEST:

Sure-footed even in the snow, Porsches always corner quickly and flatly.

PORSCHE

ANY MACHINE which is essentially different in concept pays the price of outstanding gains of performance in certain areas with unexpected losses in others. In the case of the Porsche, the major effort in the past nine year's development has been to reduce these losses rather than to extend the gains. The latter course has not been neglected, witness the Carrera, but what is to be made clear here is the sometimes subtle path of design development of this amazing car. The aim of Ferry Porsche and his father, Ferdinand, in building the original Type 356 was to supply a connoisseur's automobile, something in the Bugatti tradition of perfection. They innocently thought that a total of fifty to one hundred cars would saturate the world market for such cars! This sincere, if mistaken, belief may explain why Porsche production has always lagged behind demand. Management, even today, is incredulous at the manner in which the world, and America especially, soaks up their output. Today the story of the post-war prosperity is old stuff to us, but remember, to the Germans it came as pretty much of a surprise.

The earliest Porsches were not much more than hot-rodded, custom-bodied short-chassis Volkswagens. The connoisseurs turned out in numbers, both with money and with advice for improvements. Instead of the reduced-bore 1086 cc VW plant, it was enlarged to 1286, and, since the well-streamlined coupe body would do naught to slow the coupe, aluminum muffs were shrunk onto the VW brake drums so that they could. In 1951, the engine was further enlarged to 1488 cc, in '53 Alfin bonded aluminum-steel drums of eleven inches diameter were fitted. While making these improvements, the factory had discovered that their "Businessman's Express" wasn't half bad as a sports-racing car. Efforts in this direction soon led to a more specialized car, the Type 550 Spyder, and from this point on (1953), with but one exception, the aim was to make the 356 go *better*, not just faster. In 1955 an all-new three-piece crankcase was inaugurated, severing still another tie with the original VW. At the same time an anti-roll or "stabilizer" bar was fitted to the lower front trailing arms to reduce the Dreaded Oversteer. Previously, and some maintain subsequently too, the fastest method of pushing a Porsche around a corner involved the technique of "wischening" or wiping.

Many climbed to fame on the early Porsches, but the fact remains that a good many others thought the car was just plain squirrelly. Whether this was to cover up their personal inadequacies or not would be a rude question to pursue.

Now this anti-roll bar did not completely answer the problem at hand, namely to make the Porsche handle more like other cars, so during 1955 some more research was conducted on the *autobahnen* that nearly encircle Stuttgart and in the Alpine foothills not far to the south. As this year marked the return to the Porsche company of its pre-war building across the street, doubling working area, the changes in front end geometry were incorporated simultaneously with a major redesign of the frame-less structure's innards. This made the Type 356A, as it was now called, much more suited to series production. At the same time, the cylinder bore was increased from 80 to 82.5 mm bringing the displacement that much closer to the newly current FIA class limits. For the serious lead-foots, a detuned Spyder engine was available in the Carrera models.

Well, if the factory's aim was to eliminate "Wischening: Pro and Con" from the list of hotly debated topics among sports car initiates, they had certainly succeeded. But more

(Continued on page 59)

PORSCHE 1600 Normal Coupe

PERFORMANCE

TOP SPEED:
Two-way average .... 99 mph
Fastest one-way run .... 100 mph

ACCELERATION:
From zero to	Seconds
30 mph	5.4
40 mph	7.4
50 mph	10.7
60 mph	13.9
70 mph	18.3
Standing ¼ mile	19.5
Speed at end of quarter	72 mph

SPEED RANGES IN GEARS: (1500-5000 rpm)
I	0-24
II	14-47
III	22-74
IV	32-top

SPEEDOMETER CORRECTION:
Indicated	Actual	Indicated	Actual
30	28	60	55
40	37	70	65
50	46	80	74

FUEL CONSUMPTION:
Hard driving in 20°F. weather... 22 mpg

BRAKING EFFICIENCY:
10 successive emergency stops from 60 mph, just short of locking wheels were made at ⅔ g. More pedal pressure would lock the right rear wheel. At end of test, there was 3½ inches clearance between the floor and the bottom of the depressed pedal.

SPECIFICATIONS

POWER UNIT:
1600 Normal .... Air-cooled flat four
Valve Arrangement .... pushrod ohv, inclined exhaust valves
Bore & Stroke .... 3.25 x 2.91 in (82.5 x 74mm)
Stroke/Bore Ratio 0.89/1
Displacement .... 96.5 cu in (1582 cc)
Compression Ratio 7.5/1
Carburetion by .... Two Zenith twin-choke NDIX-32-36
Max. Power .... 60 hp (DIN) @ 4500 rpm
                             (70 bhp SAE)
Max. Torque .... 82 ft-lbs @ 2700 rpm
Idle Speed .... 700 rpm

DRIVE TRAIN:
Transmission ratios
I	3.09
II	1.76
III	1.13
IV	0.815

Final drive ratio (test car) .... 4.43 (standard)
Other available final drive ratios. 4.86, 5.18
Axle torque taken by .... gearbox case

CHASSIS:
Frame .... Pressed steel panels welded into box sections, integral with body panels
Wheelbase .... 83 in
Front Tread .... 51 in
Rear Tread .... 49 in
Suspension, front .... Trailing arms, laminated torsion bars, anti-roll bar
Suspension, rear .... Swing axles, flexible trailing arm, adjustable torsion bars
Shock absorbers .... Telescopic hydramatic
Steering type .... Z-F made Ross-type worm and roller, steering damper
Steering wheel turns L to L .. 2.7
Turning diameter .... 36 ft
Brake type .... 2LS front, single leading and trailing shoes at rear
Brake lining area .... 124 sq in
Tire size .... 5.60 x 15

GENERAL:
Length .... 155 in
Width .... 65 in
Height .... 51.5 in
Weight, test car .... 1875 lbs
Fuel capacity—U. S. gallons .... 13⅔ U. S. gallons (including 1⅓ reserve)

RATING FACTORS:
Bhp per cu in (SAE) 0.72
Bhp per sq in piston area 2.11
Torque (lb-ft per cu in) 0.85
Pounds per bhp—test car 26.8
Piston speed @ 60 mph ...... 1360 fpm
Piston speed @ max power ... 2180 fpm
Brake lining area per ton (test car) .... 132 sq in

Price $3700
Distributor .... Hoffman-Porsche Car Corp.
                             443 Park Ave.
                             New York 22, N. Y.

While engine lid's shape nicely suits window outline, access to forward plugs is cramped. However, engine removal is easy, even at home. New linkage, dual-throats are welcome features of new Zenith carburetors. Exhausts zig-zags to shrouded openings in bumper guards, like Detroit!

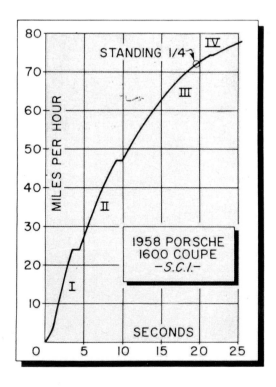

1958 PORSCHE 1600 COUPE —S.C.I.—

PORSCHE

(Continued from page 39)

than one rabid Porsche owner objected to being forcibly civilized in the name of Progress and Stability, complaining that the 356A, far from being in the Bugatti tradition, now seemed to be descended from one of W. O. Bentley's smaller lorries. When pressed for reasons, sources at Zuffenhausen took refuge behind references to the demands of the American market (!) or else insisted that this represented a real improvement in handling and was, in fact, necessary with the added power of the Carrera. Be that as it may, the Porsche-pushers at SCI all drive the earlier 1500s and like them. One thing we will admit is that the 356A series certainly rides better, being nowhere near as choppy as the Type 356s.

The 1958 1600 coupe which we have tested seems to nicely combine the best of its predecessors' advantages. The ride is comfortable and yet the steering is delightfully sensitive and light, requiring only fingertip control. Speeding down long straights with severely undulating surfaces again brings up that fascinating phenomenon of going straight on in a car which alternately points a degree or two to one side and then to the other. The value of independent rear suspension in soaking up roughness must become obvious to anyone who rides in a Porsche on bad surfaces. The wheels may go pitter-patter but the occupants are thoroughly insulated from it.

While its performance is no longer considered shattering, it certainly is a delectable car for serious cross-country touring. Though the Porsche's trunk is hardly cavernous, there is plenty of luggage space available in the back seat. The logic here seems irrefutable: if you've a back-seat passenger or two, you won't be going far because it's not *that* comfortable back there; if you haven't one, then the jump-seat may be folded to provide a wide, flat loading platform. A supplementary piece of fabric covers the gap through which small objects could fall, while a lip on the upper or forward edge of the seat back will keep parcels from sliding off under sudden braking.

Much of the well-sealed trunk itself is occupied by the spare wheel and the gas tank. The latter is to the rear, the former to the front with luggage space in the middle. Worries of ruptured gas tanks can be put to rest. The VW-like front suspension beam, the spare wheel and the welded body-frame add up to an impressively non-resilient structure in the event of a head-on collision, all of them well ahead of the gas tank. Inside, the dash board crash padding looks good but we doubt if Dr. Snively would be impressed.

Visibility is very good but in the rain it seems the wiper blades could be usefully pivoted one or two inches further outboard. The instrument panel is simple and straight forward; so much so one staff member likened it to the Henry J. (?) Keen rallyists will welcome the odometer with tenths and the speedo unit's position

(Continued on page 60)

In any season, any weather,

PORSCHE

and pleasure go together!

Remove Porsche's detachable hardtop in spring...breeze through the summer in a quick-change standard convertible top. Replace the hard-top in fall for all-winter comfort. Whether you're off to ski slope, to bathing beach, or just for the thrill of handling a dazzling road performer... Porsche makes pleasure complete!

PORSCHE

DEALERS FROM COAST TO COAST —
for name of nearest dealer write to U. S. A. Distributor:
HOFFMANN-PORSCHE CAR CORPORATION
443 PARK AVENUE · NEW YORK 22, N. Y.

SAAB

(Continued from page 52)

Leaving the Thruway, we had forty miles of twisty, treacherous road to go. We made excellent time, held up only by the few who feel the purchase price of their car entitles them to the middle half of the road. We hesitated to pass one new sedan, of a make held in considerable esteem by those who own them, because it was wallowing and sliding so badly that we were afraid he would break loose and slide into us as we passed. This fellow, with about 300 inches of displacement and almost 200 horses per passenger, was holding up our Saab!

Arriving at the approach to the ski slopes—a mile-long upgrade with a base of ice covered by several inches of snow —we were confronted by a myriad of cars in different states of immobility. We picked our way between them, frequently stopping and restarting on the slick surface. At one point, where two cars were stuck on the two-lane road, we took to the edges. The two right wheels dropped off in the deep snow, sliding us on the belly pan, but we pulled back on the road and drove up the rest of the way.

The Saab is obviously a remarkably well-built car. The gauge of the body metal is heavy, with many of the stress areas, such as at edges of the windows, welded. There is a tubular steel roll bar across the roof and each car is undercoated in sections during assembly. The dash panel is metal, stressed in such a way that it will collapse upon impact from inside the cockpit. I was told that the fiancee of a Saab engineer in Sweden slammed into the panel, leaving the imprint of her nose in the metal, but her nose didn't break! She should have taken the time to fasten the excellent and very comfortable safety belt.

Saab's safety belts fasten to the body frame; they're sturdy, not the kind that you snap on to the upholstery. The belt passes over the left shoulder of the driver (the right shoulder of the passenger), joining the buckle section that comes up from between the bucket seats. This belt secures the shoulders as well as the waist, and is installed so that it never touches the floor. It's an extra, but Saab extras come easy.

For example: How about a nice quick hop-up, for five more horses? Various size carburetor venturi inserts and high-speed jets are available, and can be changed in ten minutes by anyone who owns a wrench and a screwdriver. By installing bigger passages, the richness of the mixture is unchanged, however more of it can be introduced. Cost: two dollars for the venturi, fifty cents for the jet!

When we discussed this with Chris Custer, Saab service representative, we explored the possibilities of a man installing a high-economy setup for his wife to take shopping during the week, and on Friday night, before he packed off on a 400 mile ski trip, changing back to a larger venturi and bigger jet for more go. We asked him if this was feasible.

Chris drove into the garage and took off his tie, but he left his white shirt on, merely rolling up his sleeves. He timed the car, adjusted the points, changed the plugs, and installed and removed two or three different venturi-jet combinations. (We kept the "regular" combination for performance testing). When finished, he washed his hands and rolled down his sleeves. His shirt wasn't soiled.

However, the Saab is not designed as a do-it-yourself-service car. Timing is critical on a two-stroke engine, and unless it is hitting "on the head", fuel consumption will suffer tremendously. The Saab is timed by measuring the hundredths of a millimeter the piston is below top-dead-center. The #2 spark plug is replaced by a metal insert with a hole drilled through the center. A gauge with a rod, the same diameter as the drilled hole, seats on the insert, and the rod, hitting the top of the piston, records the *distance*. Since this method overcomes errors due to wear, it is extremely accurate.

The Saab merchandising program is built on solid service. Once a dealer is franchised, he must send a mechanic to Saab service school at Hingham, Mass. If he doesn't, he doesn't receive any more cars. This depot also stocks spares for several hundred cars, available quickly and at moderate cost. A rebuilt block, including crank, pistons and head, costs $149.50; a factory-warranted block, complete as before but also with carburetor, distributor and manifolds, costs $299.50 exchange.

All in all, the 93B incorporates an awful lot of things that most small car owners like to have in their cars. The $1895 purchase price gives you room for four full-size people, massive stowage space, heater, comfortable seats, durability, and plenty of outright economy. And if you want to race in the 750 cc class you can probably win, unless another Saab beats you.

—*Len Griffing*

PORSCHE

(Continued from page 59)

at the right.

The offending interior light has been removed from top dead center on the dash board, leaving it with a somewhat blank look. Now there are two of them, individually controlled and/or automatic, one above each door post. Sealed beams do not seem really at home in their containers either here or in the VW. The pattern ahead seems fuzzier while light to the

side is much reduced. Full positive marks for the headlight flasher button in the horn ring, an idea others should copy.

The fully reclining seats always win praise — and perhaps a few cries of surprise from the unwary. This year they are much firmer than before — less opulent, but with better lateral support. This pleased most yet annoyed others. Leg room can still be a bit of a problem for the driver. Here's how. Though the long seat travel assures plenty of fore and aft room (is there any other car where a six footer can't even reach the toe board?), the driver's left foot has only a small space for resting and even this is too far to the right.

PORSCHE

(Continued from page 60)

quickly clears it.

Noise, also a serious problem on air-cooled engines, is combatted by many layers of insulation. Though adequately subdued, it's still noticeable.

Engine accessibility, as before, is great for minor operations but a real pain in the neck for changing spark plugs and adjusting valves. The latter involves lying on the ground and there's not much that can be done about it. But why can't the engine lid be made larger, especially at the forward end? Reaching the forward two plugs takes an acquired knack and the only solace is that it's tougher on a Carrera (twin ignition and the same lid.)

Otherwise, maintenance is a snap. Greasing involves but twelve fittings on the trailing like i.f.s. and the unequally divided track rod steering (every 1500 miles) with rarer attention to clutch and hand-brake cables.

Brakes scored highly on our test. Though helped in avoiding fade by the extreme cold, they *are* good brakes and well predate domestic efforts in the same direction. The Porsche's drums are of aluminum which is cast onto a ferrous braking surface (and a splined hub, at the rear). Similar, if not identical, to Fairchild's Alfin process, there is an intermolecular bond between the two metals which gives additional strength and better heat conductivity than the Buick system of cast-in dowels.

Bumpers are much in the European tradition being lightly made of thin gauge body steel. Their weakness in American parking traditions is overcome by an extensive system of bumper guards and bars. Ideal for hanging badges on though, if pure aerodynamics bore you.

It's very hard to write a road test on a car which has remained essentially the same for so long, especially when you've been driving one of them yourself for three years. So I will add a purely personal note, full perhaps of prejudices. I like my '54 Super coupe very much indeed (although roller-bearing crankshaft *are* expensive) and I probably will continue to drive it for quite a while longer. But the improvements of the '58 are indeed tempting, especially since the car handles so much more lightly and smoothly than all the 1600s which preceded it. Porsches have always been delectable motor cars, and in this one they have reached a new peak. If you've ever liked the Porsche before, then I can recommend the '58s without reservation. If you demand more acceleration than is offered by this model, then the new Supers (which no longer have roller cranks) appear to be very good bets, although at a hefty price increase for a power-pack. Those who feel Porsches are too expensive should give one a careful looking over to realize the amount of value received.

If you pride yourself on knowing your way around sports cars, then you owe it to yourself to try a Porsche.

Stephen F. Wilder

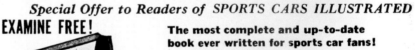

CAR AND DRIVER ROAD TEST

PORSCHE 911 S

"This is no car for a novice," warns a Porsche brochure.
All told, the admonition is a bit gratuitous.

Oversteer is back—and Porsche's got it! Early Porsches had it too, and now it has come full circle. Barely three years ago, Porsche employed a device called a "camber compensator" to curb the oversteering tendencies of the 356 series. Then the completely redesigned suspension of the 911 and 912 models made Porsches behave like normal, front-engined cars, and the purists started to carp. Porsche had even hidden an iron weight behind the 912's front bumper to keep the back end from coming around. Sure, understeer is safe—great for the masses—but oversteer makes driving fun . . . if you're expert enough to handle it. Fanciers of the marque yearned for the good old days when they used to *wischen* their Speedsters through turns, tails all hung out, arms sawing away like mad on the steering wheel.

Porsche is making a car for these drivers again, offering a sportier version of the 6-cylinder 911 dubbed the 911S. S for Super. Super because horsepower is up 20%, from 148 to 180. Super because the brake discs are vented. And Super because the suspension has been modified with strengthened struts, Koni adjustable shocks, a stiffer front anti-sway bar, and an anti-sway bar added at the rear.

The rear anti-sway bar, in addition to reducing body lean, has an effect diametrically opposed to that of the old "camber compensator." *Gott im Himmel! Übersteuer!* We'll hang out our tails on the Siegfried Line. "This is no car for a novice," warns a Porsche brochure.

The 911S's introduction has occasioned a shuffle in Porsche's marketing structure so that it now approximates the former ascending scale of Normal, Super and Carrera engines in the same body. The prices have been rearranged too. On the bottom

CONTINUED 37

19

For a 2-liter sports car, a quarter-mile in 15.2 sec. at 92 mph ranks with building a replica of the Great Pyramid of Cheops overnight.

rung is the 102-hp, 4-cylinder 912, with a base price of $4790, up $100 from last year, but two instrument panel gauges have been added. The 148-hp, 6-cylinder 911 is now $5990, *down* $500 from last year. However, many items that were standard on the 911 in '66 are optional in '67. In effect, it becomes simply a higher-powered version of the 912. The flagship of the fleet, the $6990, 180-hp, 6-cylinder 911S, is loaded with performance, luxury, and distinctive features like racy-looking forged magnesium-alloy wheels, a leather-covered steering wheel rim, extra instrumentation, an auxiliary gasoline heater, fog lights, pile carpets, and waffled padding on the dash. Most of these unique options are available—for a price—on the 911 and 912 (the mag wheels for $175), along with the old standbys like chromed steel road wheels.

In our zeal to obtain a 911S for a road test, we had to settle for one right off the boat. The car hadn't been dealer-prepared, much less fine-tuned, and it wasn't exactly in full song. Acceleration times were little better than those of a Weber-carbureted 911 5-speed we drove recently, which clocked 0-60 mph in 6.9 seconds and the standing quarter-mile in 15.6 seconds at 90 mph. Actually, our times were nearly identical to those claimed for the 911S by Porsche. The German government requires car manufacturers to certify performance which can be duplicated by any production model straight off the showroom floor. The factory figures are therefore ultra-conservative and represent the slowest car within assembly-line tolerances. Careful tuning of a 911S with some mileage on it should hack close to a second off our 0-60 mph

time of 6.5 seconds. Still, neither that, nor a quarter-mile in 15.2 seconds at 92 mph (with three gears yet to go) is bad for *any* high-performance car. For a little 2-liter sports car, it ranks with Robert Moses building a replica of the Great Pyramid of Cheops overnight.

The brakes on our test car left something to be desired, although—again—were enormously above average. The 911 and 912 have Ate-Dunlop solid discs on all four wheels; the 911S's discs have internal radial venting. Vented discs are new to Porsche; so new, in fact, that Porsche has mistakenly laid claim to building the first sports car thus equipped. The Corvette Sting Ray has had vented discs since 1965, at which time Chevrolet claimed to be first with drums inside the rear discs for the parking/emergency brake. Porsche had had *that* feature since

CONTINUED

Within normal driving
limits, and with reasonable
caution, the 911S handles
head and shoulders
above practically
everything else on the road.

1964, so perhaps the current German boast is just Porsche's way of
getting back at Chevy.

At any rate, the bugs aren't yet
out of Porsche's vented discs. True,
they run cooler, making them less
prone to fade, and lengthening pad
life, but they are more difficult to
modulate. If Ford's experience with
vented discs on their Le Mans-win-
ning Mk. II is any indication, the
problem may be that the discs aren't
dimensionally and/or geometrically
stable. In our 80-0 mph braking
test, the left rear wheel would in-
variably lock up, and the shortest
stopping distance we could record
was 271 ft. (.71G). Not half bad,
but we knew the car could do better. Later, we sampled another
911S, and, after heating up the rather hard pads, it stopped from 80
mph in 242 ft. (.88G), but we have
stopped a solid-disc 911 in 218 ft.
(.98G), which is more like what the
true potential is.

Normally, we measure a car's cornering power by clocking lap times
on a skid pad of a known radius. We
don't use an accelerometer, or Tap-
ley meter, because it adds the vehicle's roll angle to the absolute lateral acceleration, and there is no
accurate way to distinguish between
the two. (Similarly, on braking and
acceleration, the vehicle's pitch angle is automatically included in the
reading.) However, during one
phase of this test, we had the opportunity to ride shotgun with expert
Porsche pilot Lake Underwood as he
booted the 911S around a road circuit. Out of curiosity, we installed a
lateral accelerometer to measure the
911S's cornering power. On level,
unbanked turns, the instrument
showed a maximum reading of .93G
on right-hand corners, and .89G on
left-hand bends. Subtracting a generous 9° (.10G) for roll angle, the
911S's limit of controllability is well
over .81G.

The 911S's oversteer characteristic
appears early in the car's cornering
range. At low lateral accelerations,
it understeers mildly. From .40G on
up, less and less steering lock is
(Text continued on Page 91;
Specifications overleaf)

JULIUS WEITMANN

PORSCHE 911S

Importer: Porsche of America Corp.
107 Tryon Ave. West
Teaneck, N.J.

Number of dealers in U.S.: 244

Vehicle type: Rear-engine, rear-wheel-drive, 2+2-passenger GT car

Price as tested: $7,255 (Manufacturer's suggested retail price, plus Federal excise tax, dealer preparation and delivery charges; does not include state and local taxes, license or freight charges)

Options on test car: AM-FM radio ($180.00)

ENGINE

Type: Air-cooled flat six, aluminum block, 12-port aluminum heads, 8 main bearings
Bore x stroke............3.15 x 2.60 in, 80 x 66 mm
Displacement............121.5 cu in, 1991 cc
Compression ratio............9.8 to one
Carburetion......2 x 3-bbl Weber 46 IDA 3Cs
Valve gear......Single overhead camshafts on each bank, chain-driven, rocker arms
Power (SAE)............180 bhp @ 6600 rpm
Torque (SAE)............144 lbs/ft @ 5200 rpm
Specific power output......1.48 bhp/cu in, 90.5 bhp/liter
Max. recommended engine speed...7200 rpm

DRIVE TRAIN

Transmission:.....5-speed manual, all-synchro
Clutch diameter............8.46 in
Final drive ratio............4.43 to one

Gear	Ratio	Mph/1000 rpm	Max. test speed
I	3.09	5.3	38 mph (7200 rpm)
II	1.89	8.8	63 mph (7200 rpm)
III	1.32	12.5	89 mph (7200 rpm)
IV	1.04	15.9	114 mph (7200 rpm)
V	0.79	20.9	140 mph (6700 rpm)

DIMENSIONS AND CAPACITIES

Wheelbase............87.1 in
Track............F:53.4 in, R:52.2 in
Length............163.9 in
Width............63.4 in
Height............52.0 in
Ground clearance............5.9 in
Curb weight............2279 lbs
Test weight............2535 lbs
Weight distribution, F/R............41/59%
Lbs/bhp (test weight)............14.0
Battery capacity............12 volts, 45 amp/hr
Alternator capacity............420 watts
Fuel capacity............16.4 gal
Oil capacity............9.5 qts

SUSPENSION

F: Ind., MacPherson strut with lower wishbone, longitudinal torsion bars, anti-sway bar, Koni adjustable shock absorbers
R: Ind., semi-trailing links, transverse torsion bars, anti-sway bar, Koni adjustable shock absorbers

STEERING

Type............Rack and pinion
Turns lock-to-lock............2.75
Turning circle............34 ft

BRAKES

F: Ate-Dunlop 11.1-in. vented discs
R: Ate-Dunlop 11.25-in. vented discs with integral 7.09-in. drums for handbrake
Swept area............371.0 sq in

WHEELS AND TIRES

Wheel size and type:............4.5J x 15-in, aluminum alloy, 5-bolt
Tire make, size and type..Dunlop HR 165-15 SP radial-ply, tube-type
Test inflation pressures...F: 32 psi, R: 35 psi
Tire load rating:.....810 lbs per tire @ 24 psi

PERFORMANCE

Zero to	Seconds
30 mph	2.2
40 mph	3.4
50 mph	4.8
60 mph	6.5
70 mph	9.0
80 mph	11.4
90 mph	14.6
100 mph	18.2

Standing ¼-mile............15.2 sec @ 92 mph
80-0 mph............271 ft (.71 G)
Fuel mileage......14-18 mpg on premium fuel
Cruising range............230-296 m

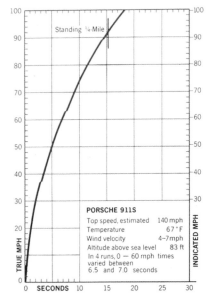

PORSCHE 911S

Top speed, estimated 140 mph
Temperature 67° F
Wind velocity 4–7 mph
Altitude above sea level 83 ft
In 4 runs, 0 — 60 mph times varied between 6.5 and 7.0 seconds

CHECK LIST

ENGINE
Starting............Fair
Response............Excellent
Vibration............Excellent
Noise............Fair

DRIVE TRAIN
Shift linkage............Very Good
Synchro action............Excellent
Clutch smoothness............Excellent
Transmission noise............Excellent

STEERING
Effort............Very Good
Response............Excellent
Road feel............Excellent
Kickback............Very Good

SUSPENSION
Ride comfort............Good
Roll resistance............Very Good
Pitch control............Very Good
Harshness control............Good

HANDLING
Directional control............Very Good
Predictability............Very Good
Evasive maneuverability............Excellent
Resistance to sidewinds............Fair

BRAKES
Pedal pressure............Very Good
Response............Excellent
Fade resistance............Excellent
Directional control............Excellent

CONTROLS
Wheel position............Excellent
Pedal position............Very Good
Gearshift position............Good
Relationship............Excellent
Small controls............Good

INTERIOR
Ease of entry/exit............Good
Noise level (cruising)............Good
Front seating comfort............Excellent
Front leg room............Excellent
Front head room............Very Good
Front hip/shoulder room............Good
Rear seating comfort............Poor
Rear leg room............Poor
Rear head room............Poor
Rear hip/shoulder room............Poor
Instrument comprehensiveness....Excellent
Instrument legibility............Excellent

VISION
Forward............Excellent
Front quarter............Very Good
Side............Excellent
Rear quarter............Fair
Rear............Fair

WEATHER PROTECTION
Heater/defroster............Excellent
Ventilation............Fair
Weather sealing............Very Good

CONSTRUCTION QUALITY
Sheet metal............Excellent
Paint............Excellent
Chrome............Very Good
Upholstery............Excellent
Padding............Very Good
Hardware............Very Good

GENERAL
Headlight illumination............Good
Parking and signal lights............Excellent
Wiper effectiveness............Very Good
Service accessibility............Fair
Trunk space............Fair
Interior storage space............Good
Bumper protection............Fair

(continued from page 39)
needed to keep this car on a given course. By .70G, it's in a full-blooded four-wheel drift, and the steering behavior is back-tracking toward neutral-steer. Beyond the limit of the tires' rolling adhesion, the 911S reacts like any car with a rearward weight bias, and spins, or, if you're quick enough to catch it, power-slides like an old dirt-track roadster. All told, Porsche's admonition, "not for the novice" is a bit gratuitous. Within normal driving limits and with reasonable caution, the 911S handles predictably, controllably, and head and shoulders above practically anything else on the road.

There's always room for improvement, however, and the present limitations on the 911S's absolute cornering power are imposed by its wheels and tires. We were stunned to learn that the rim width of those flashy new wheels is still only 4½ inches, a mere half-inch wider than a Volkswagen's, and unchanged since Porsche went from 16-in. to 15-in. wheels in the dim dawn of time. Four-and-a-half inches was unfashionably skinny even then, and is almost inconceivable today. Porsche ballyhoos the notion that their racing program improves the breed of their production cars, but the competition-bred lesson of the benefits of wide-rim wheels has apparently gone unheeded. One-inch wider rims alone would have wrought as much improvement in the car's handling ability as all their tricks with rear anti-sway bars, stiffer shocks and spring rates, and radial-ply tires. Wide-rim racing wheels are available from Porsche for competition drivers, and American Racing Equipment in San Francisco is doing a land-office business in 5- and 6-in. mag wheels for disc-braked Porsches. The introduction of Porsche's own mag wheel would have been an ideal opportunity to cash in on the trend, but Stuttgart fumbled the ball. We can only surmise that steps will soon be taken to correct this state of affairs. In the meantime, it is of some consolation that the new wheels aid brake heat dissipation and reduce unsprung weight.

The 911S's radial-ply tires, German Dunlop SPs, are the other limiting factor. Radial-ply tires are generally advantageous, developing a higher cornering force at a lower slip angle than conventional tires. They do this by keeping more rubber on the road through a softer lateral compliance—the tread stays flat

on the ground while the sidewall rolls. This gives radials an odd feel; they mush sideways until the slack is taken up, then they grip. The SPs, in particular, have an odd tread pattern, like a knobby snow tire, with S-shaped cleats and a deep (¼-inch) tread depth. The cleats are so tall that they bend like willows under side loads. Coupled with the normal mushiness of radials, the SPs give a sensation somewhat akin to riding on bristles. It would be interesting to try a 911S with a shallow-tread radial-ply tire, like the Michelin X, or an American high-performance tire, like the Firestone Wide Oval.

The only real handling *fault* of the 911S is a corkscrewing motion of the front end when cornering on an undulating surface. This appears to be a by-product of the Porsche's unconventional MacPherson strut front suspension. There is no loss of adhesion or directional stability, but with a lack of other vices it stood out disconcertingly.

If we've dwelled on the 911S's handling traits, it's because they are the most obvious departure from the standard 911, impressing us far more than the 32 extra horsepower. The 180-hp engine is notable mainly for its lack of temperament. Its idle is slightly more uneven, it accelerates with a more vigorous growl, prefers super-premium fuel, and consumes it a shade more prodigally than the 911. The power and torque curves aren't "peaky," and, except for an ill-advised change in gearing, it pulls as well from low revs. Revving it beyond its 7200 rpm redline would be all too easy were it not for a centrifugal ignition governor concealed in the distributor arm.

With racing versions of Porsche's flat-six pulling close to 235 horsepower, raising the output of the street engine to 180 horsepower was easy—a matter of subtle changes in the cam timing and carburetor jetting (Webers are used on all 6-cylinder Porsches now), plus an increase in compression ratio from 9.0- to 9.8-to-one. Initial reports indicate that there is less carbon build-up with the higher compression ratio. Oil control appears to be difficult even on the 148-hp engine, however, with most owners reporting 400-500 miles per quart. The dry sump holds nearly two gallons, so topping up could be a matter of every other gas stop.

The original 911 had a long, 2.83 first gear, which made the car hard to start from rest. To ease the load on the clutch, first gear on all

Porsches has been shortened to 3.09, with the other gears closed up in suit. The 911 and 912 have .86 high gears while the 911S has a .79 high gear, enabling its engine to wind the car out to its full top-speed potential of 140 mph. Unfortunately, this has resulted in a wider gap between fourth and fifth gears, and a 20% loss of pulling power in high. A gearchange is necessary for surprisingly mild hills. Since nobody in his right mind should think the unthinkable—140 mph on our public highways—a shorter fifth gear would mean less rowing back-and-forth on the gearshift lever. We really didn't mind more frequent use of the transmission, though; slicing through the Porsche's gears remains one of the great delights of the Western Hemisphere.

Little else is changed from the 911 of our April, 1965 Road Research Report. The styling still looks good to us, and, like any Porsche, it has personality in its design, workmanship, and its seat-of-the-pants telegraphy about what it's doing. The firmer ride heightens this sensation, although thankfully, the increase in stiffness has not been accompanied by a similar increase in harshness. Sidewind sensitivity, already a tender subject with 911 owners, is, if anything, slightly worse in the 911S, although hardly noticeable below a thoroughly illegal 120 mph.

Maybe it's just us, but, in retrospect, the steering wheel seems oversized, giving more leverage than needed on one of the easiest-steering cars built today. Also, we note that an optional spacer can bring the wheel 1½-inches closer to the driver, which we think we'd prefer. Otherwise, the interior is a model for the way all cars should be built—sports cars or utility sedans, front-engined or rear, Detroit or Kharkov. The seats, upholstered in a new air-flow weaving, stay cooler, and, as always, are almost infinitely adjustable to a variety of comfortable positions. There's plenty of room (except, perhaps, elbow room), and all the controls are located where you can get at them easily and operate them efficiently.

Just cruising around town or belting along back roads like a would-be racer, the 911S is a great way for getting from Point A to Point B, even when Point B represented only an excuse to drive somewhere.

Each successive Porsche has been the ultimate Porsche, which is akin to its being the ultimate luxury GT car. The 911S surely must be the all-time high. Where can Porsche go from here? Build a car with disappearing headlights? **C/D**

The Speedster is Dead; Long Live the Speedster!

Love Affair With a Bathtub

BY JOHN JEROME

• A couple of years ago Hollywood produced a movie called *Harper*. It starred Paul Newman as a down-at-the-heels private eye who got slugged around a lot, but persevered, and the critics loved it. They said it was a return to the good old days of Humphrey Bogart's "Sam Spade" character, twitted the whole super-technical James Bond mystique, and generally provided the public with the good, clean, cops-and-robbers kind of fun.

I don't know about any of that. All I know is that this character Harper, when he wasn't getting beaten to a pulp by the bad guys or trying to put the make on big-eyed old Janet Leigh, was driving around in the most clapped-out, disreputable, tired-looking Porsche Speedster I ever saw. A real, old, rotty-looking Speedster. It was painted a faded-out blue-gray, and had great camouflage spots of red-lead primer all over one side; and—horror of horrors—the top was almost always up, which is about the worst thing you could possibly do to a Speedster. Moreover, in an unusual burst of *cinéma vérité* for Hollywood, they used the actual growling sounds of the Porsche, instead of some phony, slick-sounding motor dubbed into the sound track. So the doors did clunk just right, and the engine would occasionally cough back through the carburetors the way a Speedster would when the carburetor float levels were a little off. I remember I came out of that movie without the first clue to what had gone on in the plot, but lost in a wistful reminiscence about Porsches lost and gone forever from my own automotive time. I've never seen Hollywood do a better piece of casting—not Paul Newman as Harper, but the Porsche Speedster as the car he drove. . . .

The staple items in an enthusiast's diet come and go, and I have no idea what a real hotblood drives now. I mean the fellow for whom *the* ownership of *the* vehicle wipes out all other considerations—supplants material success and making it with ladies and Finding Himself. A motorcycle, I suppose, or a Shelby Mustang with mag wheels.

But for a while there, it was a Porsche. The MG-TC of song and story supposedly started it all over here after the war, but not many people ever actually *owned* one. A lot more owned later-model MGs, and various Triumphs, and *believed* in Morgans and things like that. Near the end of the Great Sports Car Thing, Lotus Sevens had a lot of status, but nobody ever really owned them, especially not to drive on the street, which was the major part of the whole business.

I suspect that while all those people were driving MGs and Triumphs, and believing in Morgans and Lotus Sevens, what they all really wanted was a Porsche Speedster. It was the Right Car, for a period of about five years, from 1954 to 1959. Is it now a "classic"? Whether or not the Speedster fits that pseudo-exalted classification requires a tedious definition and all that junk, and I'm sure most Speedster owners couldn't care less. I've never seen a Speedster re-

Joiner's Speedster has a '66 engine brought up to SC specifications— then bored and stroked to two liters—by Vic Meinhardt of Long Island. Engine is ported and relieved. Burch exhaust system, sodium-cooled exhaust valves, a Stewart-Warner electric fuel pump, Carrera clutch, CBAB transmission ratios— the works. For gymkhanas, it has a limited-slip and a specially fitted between-the-seats Volkswagen handbrake with the ratchet removed so that it can't be locked into place. The front end is all 1961 Porsche, with the ZF steering gearbox. Rear is decambered 1½°, fitted with a camber compensator spring. Goodyear Sports Car Special LW's, with the R4 tread pattern, are used.

Love Affair
With a
Bathtub

(continued)

*It was ruby red when
it was delivered in
August, 1957, to a GI
stationed in France. It
was gold, once, and white
at least twice. But an
art director named
Jim Joiner decided it
had to be black. He
took it down to bare metal,
then put on 14 loving
coats of lacquer to
make it look like this.
The factory managed to
dig up new replacement
hardware for everything
except the hood handle
—this one's from a
Convertible D. Then Jim
saw some neat nerfing
bars on California
Porsches and abandoned
forever the idea of just
a "mint" restoration;
the nerf bars looked too
right. Who ever heard
of a stock Speedster?*

stored to anything like pristine, mint, perfect, absolutely original condition, and I don't think anybody'd bother. There are too many interesting things to change on them, too many new "improvements" to play with.

But I do know Speedsters are getting restored like crazy, and I suspect it is as fun cars rather than as show cars. Porsche buffs discovered, a few years ago, that Speedster bodies in anything like decent condition were going the way of the carrier pigeon; sports car racing was siphoning them off the market and wrecking them in large numbers. The MG-TC restoration craze ran out its own string some time ago, and now, by the immutable laws of supply and demand, the Speedster market is beginning to climb rapidly. I'm not sure there's a fortune to be made yet in trading in Speedster futures, but the price *is* going up.

The first time I really lusted after a Speedster, you could buy one delivered in Odessa, Tex., for $2995. Chrysler Windsors—the ones with the great, long, straight-line tail fins—were selling for something like $2760, for which money you got about 20 feet more car, infinite complication, and not quite as much performance. I did not buy the Speedster, and somehow I've always thought that that incredible length of Chrysler—which I didn't buy either—talked me out of it. That was probably my last act of automotive sanity.

When I finally got around to owning a Speedster, most of the street versions were pretty well clapped-out. I bought mine in 1960 with the mechanical parts in a box, paid $750 for it, put $3000 worth of parts into it, drove it for two years, and never had as much pleasure from a car before or since. I sold it—running this time, not yet back in a cardboard carton—for $750; the $3000 I lost on parts in the transaction was the best investment I ever made.

The finances didn't have anything to do with it, however. What counted with the Speedster was what it was: an ugly little bathtub of a car that was dirt simple, bordered on the unbreakable, and went like stink. I suppose it must be considered terribly obsolete now, and the flaws in design were pretty ridiculously evident even in its own time. The rear end was much too heavy. The car oversteered like crazy until you started fiddling with it. Clutch cables broke occasionally, clutches burned out regularly and throttle linkages fell off often (at any one of at least 12 different connection points that I can remember offhand). The oil radiator, hidden inside the fan shrouding, would sometimes develop copious leaks, and it was easier but messier to keep adding oil than to tear the engine apart to get to the oil cooler. The leak also assured—for those lucky enough to have a later model Speedster with defrosters—a thin, vaporous coating of engine oil all over the inside of the windshield.

You overlooked those things. You liked the way the doors and hinges worked (I haven't owned a Porsche for five years, but I can still shut my eyes and hear the sound of the door shutting). You liked the way the car was so all-of-a-piece that nothing ever rattled (although with a unit body and an air-cooled engine you never lacked for what the British were wont to call the Porsche's "characteristic, flat, thrumming exhaust note"). You liked the screwball handling, so easy to dirt-track around, so easy to get onto, and so capable of convincing you that you were really pretty fast after all.

So you started learning the tricks. The first thing you did was decamber the rear wheels, going to negative camber in an attempt to alleviate the oversteer. You learned to carry five to seven pounds more air pressure in the rear tires than in the front, for the same reason. You sealed off the carburetor heaters, and removed all that useless hardware from the engine shrouding. (A clean floor in the engine compartment was the first sign of a hip Porsche owner.) You stopped

73

trusting the car to ordinary mechanics, and learned to do *everything* yourself. (Anyway, authorized Porsche mechanics were always telling you that if you did all that stuff you'd no longer have the manageable, smooth-running car the Speedster was intended to be. They didn't understand that you didn't *want* a manageable, smooth-running, etc.) In short, you fiddled. It was an infinitely fiddle-able car.

I have to admit that the night after I saw that movie *Harper*, I lay awake for a couple of hours, assembling and disassembling Porsche parts in my mind. I was never much of a mechanic, but the Speedster was, in its oddball way, so absolutely straightforward and sensible that it managed to withstand even my mechanical idiocy.

Basically, it was just a souped-up Volkswagen with different sheet metal. On top of a metal platform, Porsche placed a sort of inverted soup-bowl of a body, with a hole cut out for the cockpit. A *large* hole. The suspension was mostly made up of Volkswagen pieces with the VW parts numbers machined off (so you had to pay Porsche's price for replacements): trailing links with torsion bars at the front, swing axles with torsion bars at the back. Also at the back were the air-cooled flat-four engine and gearbox, developed from VW parts originally, later Porsche's own. And all that stuff was bolted to this floor-and-body combination that made a welded-up box-within-a-barrel, rigid as Hoover Dam. You could pull the engine in an hour, put it back in two, pull engine *and* transmission in about four hours. (The original Porsche workshop manual called for three workmen to remove the transmission. One guy went underneath and undid all the bolts. Then the other two guys lowered the transmission onto his belly, caught an axle in one hand and an ankle in the other, and pulled everything out from under the car. Straightforward.)

Just as the Volkswagen was the starting place for the Speedster, the Speedster you bought was only the starting place for what you eventually drove. Getting absolute satisfaction out of the car was a case of learning all the secrets, secrets generally stumbled onto by the California experimentalists, like Racer Brown and Ed Barker. Those secrets then spread eastward like what must have seemed, to the Authorized Porsche Service types, an insidious plague.

If you had a 1500cc Speedster you could bring it up to 1600cc simply by putting the 1600cc cylinder barrels and pistons on it—but only if you had a three-piece crankcase. If you had a post-'57 Speedster, it had cast-iron barrels, which could actually be bored out—but there was a problem in getting oversized pistons. Pre-'58 cars had chrome-plated aluminum barrels which never wore out, supposedly—but when they did you had to have them re-plated by a West Coast specialty shop, or a shop that could re-chrome aircraft cylinder barrels. The pre-'58 cars also had two single-throat Solex carburetors, the later ones had two double-throat Zeniths. Naturally, there were differences about which was better for top-end power, etc., just as there were aesthetic differences of opinion about whether or not the pre-'58's double-button tail lights were prettier than the '58's teardrop tail lights.

And then there were the transmissions. Porsche owner's manual had a page in them with a fascinating chart showing the possible speed ranges of all the possible gearbox ratios. The available gearing was classified in A, B, and C ratios, with A being the low end and C the high. If you had, for example, a B first gear, a B second, an A third, and a B fourth, you said you had "BBAB" gears. There was an A, a B, and a C ratio for each gear—and the top three gears were all interchangeable!

Thus the fun began. Everyone wanted something other than what came with the car.

(Continued on page 84)

Love Affair With a Bathtub

(continued)

Above and center: ex-Porsche owner Jerome tries two-Porsche owner Joiner's car (he also has a coupe), and comes away with a wistful look in his eyes. Lower left: Joiner tells Jerome some of his secrets. Lower right: the infamous top in all its evil glory. Joiner didn't intend to do a complete restoration, originally. He was using the car for club races and gymkhanas, and merely decided that the interior was getting a bit tatty, so he'd bring that up to snuff. One thing led to another. Now, he's got just about the most gorgeous Porsche Speedster in the world, and the interior—where it all started—is about to need redoing again. Where will it all end?

CAR and DRIVER

LOVE AFFAIR WITH A BATHTUB

(continued from page 75)

There were adherents to the BBAB concept, proselytizers for CCAA, and so on. The search was always for special purposes, or special driving habits. You might want, for instance, to design your gearbox to have a stump-puller to start in, good punch in the intermediate ranges, and as much acceleration as possible in top. In short, a short-course car: BBAA. (Nobody I knew ever actually had an A first gear.) For more top end, go to BBAB, or BBBC, etc.

Every Speedster owner had his own list of secrets, of every conceivable kind, for every component. As far as I know there were really only eight series-produced Speedsters, the 1300cc "Normal" and "Super," and the "Normal," "Super," and "Carrera" models in both 1500 and 1600cc sizes; although, apparently, fewer than 100 1300 Speedsters were ever made. Total Speedster production was pegged at 4953 by the factory.

The Normal engines were basically big-displacement, two-carburetor Volkswagen engines. The Supers were Normals hotted up by the usual routes. (Plus the addition, in the 1300 and 1500cc version, of the vaunted Hirth roller-bearing crankshaft, which, according to legend, used to gall at the drop of a hat, or 500 rpm, whichever came first. It absolutely could *not* be lugged.) The Carreras had dohc on both banks, at least a half-dozen jackshafts to turn the cams.

Eight series-produced Speedsters did not mean eight mechanical combinations, however. Porsche was never loathe to make an improvement during production, and I doubt there are very many people who really know which changes were made to which cars at which time. The precedent for fiddling with the car started at the factory; by the time the car got to the individual owner, it was practically congenital. It's possible that the factory did, at some time, turn out at least two Speedsters that were alike in every detail—but they didn't stay that way very long.

In 1959 Porsche dropped the Speedster for the Convertible D, which had a taller windshield, a more civilized top, and roll-up windows—and 300 pounds more weight. Speedster buffs wept. For at least three years afterward, while we all cried that the Convertible D really wasn't much of a race car, brand new Speedsters kept turning up mysteriously from the factory. I must have met 12 different fellows, each of whom told me that he had gotten the last—the absolute *last*—Speedster that Porsche ever made. They may still be making them, for all I know.

Talk of the Convertible D brings us—heels dragging—to the subject of the infamous Speedster top. Some far-gone Porscheophiles finally managed to convince themselves that the basic Speedster, top down, was reasonably good-looking. I even suffered that aberration myself. But *nobody* was ever able

to say any good words for the appearance of the car with the top up. Erect the top, and suddenly the car looked like two men in a horse costume at a masquerade ball—a recognizable shape on each end, but a squirming, lumpy mass, inadequately covered with some spurious, flimsy material, in the middle.

It was a simple enough structure, that top, a collection of hoops with a canvas layer (thin), just like other tops. It worked so well, so easily, that I've often reached back from the driver's seat while waiting for a light to change, pulled it up and forward, and latched it in a matter of seconds.

There was plenty of headroom inside. Unfortunately, what went up to provide headroom must come down to meet the low windshield at the front. And for side curtains there were only six-inch slits over the doors. The effect from the outside was positively sinister—the narrow windows front and side made the car look like a miniature tank; it seemed to need machine guns poking out of the slits. The effect from the inside was to turn a racy little sports car into a dank Orgone box.

Even with the top down and the sun shining, the Speedster tended to be a bit all-enveloping, because of the seating position. Speedster seats were the true origin of the term "bucket"—never mind what you heard about those metal devices in C-47's. Porsche seats were *hard*, with padding confined almost entirely to the seat—and driver—

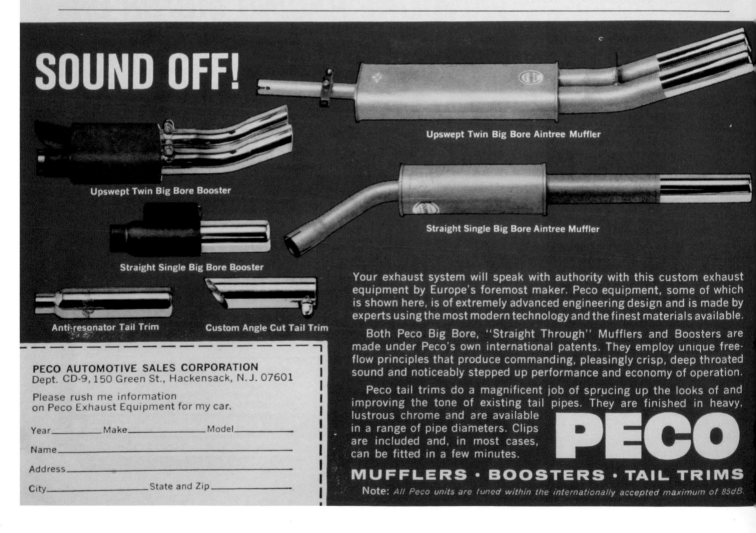

bottom. What's more, they were sharply wedge-shaped, so that an expansive rear had to be literally driven into the seat.

But, surprisingly enough, they were comfortable. Raked far back, with good support under the thighs and around the kidneys, the body weight nicely balanced between lower back and buttocks, the seats were, after the first shock, marvelous for long distance driving. Because the sides were curved well up, and the bucket itself so wedge-shaped, a seat belt was unnecessary for lateral location.

The first time I got my Speedster running, I put 50 slow miles on the engine that I'd guessed and fumbled back together, and then a friend and I jumped into it at midnight and set out to go watch a race 660 miles away. It was March, in Texas, and there was a minor dust storm blowing when we left. We made 20 miles before the throttle linkage fell off and the engine conked out.

After a half-hour of reassembly and head-scratching speculation, we determined that the main tank had run dry (no fuel gauge, but a VW-type reserve), and we were simply out of gas; in the meantime we had absolutely fried the starter motor, grinding away with a stiff engine. We push-started, made it to a gas station, and continued on our way.

Two days later we were home, having driven over 1300 miles without ever putting the top up—cold, dirty, sunburned, and absolutely in love with the Speedster.

I kept the Speedster for two years, and drove it over 60,000 miles, which was about the mileage it had already registered when I bought it. I prepared it and raced it a few times, with reasonable success. I commuted to a job 30 miles from home in it daily for nine months. I painted it once, and repaired some of my own stupidity in the engine internals once, but mostly I just drove it. It was eternally a soft, easy car to drive: light steering, easy controls, long and sloppy throws in the gearbox, absolute roomy comfort in the interior. I moved to Colorado for awhile, and had it in the mountains for a time before I sold it. That was very nice.

I didn't weep when I got rid of it. The flywheel was working loose on the crankshaft (which I didn't know, but the resulting mechanical knock terrified me), and I let the car go with a huge sigh of relief because the time and the place to get back into it and set it right just weren't available any longer. I can't even say I wish I had it now; the time and place still aren't available.

But then I don't expect, ever, to get that kind of satisfaction from a car again. What appealed to me most about the Speedster was its solidity, its integrity. I never refrained from going anywhere or doing anything that I thought was possible in a car, just because I didn't want to risk the Speedster. I drove it on and off roads, through pastures and across ditches, pounded at 75 mph down potholed dirt roads in it, raced it, spun it, stalled it, over-revved it, chased rabbits with it, did every bloody silly thing to it that can be done to a car except flip it, and it never betrayed me once. There was never a time when the bobble couldn't be traced to my own excesses, beyond the absolute—and recognizable—limits of that car. No other car I ever owned was so generous.

When *C/D* told me that they'd found this restored Speedster, and would I go talk to the guy and drive it and write about it, well, it took me a good thirteen-hundredths of a second to make up my mind to accept. So I went up to Connecticut on a gorgeous spring day, and met Jim Joiner, and we stood around in the sunshine and talked about the car. I crawled all over it, and then we took it out and blasted up and down back roads for a couple of hours, seeing what it was like. It was really splendid, lovingly and tastefully restored, and at the same time—in the tradition—lovingly modified. I even put the top up and drove it a half-mile or so, listening to how all the sounds change.

It was a lot different from my car, in thousands of ways. Much stronger—the California guys have learned a lot more, and so has Porsche, in the past nine years. They're miles beyond what we used to do to *our* Speedsters. But underneath, it was still the squat little box-in-a-barrel. The door hinges, and the crazy dead spaces under the floorboards, and all that—in the nooks and crannies, it was like coming home. It sounded tougher, and handled better, and went faster, but it was all the same. The throttle linkage even fell off twice while we were playing with the car.   C/D

Preview Test: Porsche 914·914/6

The Speedster concept lives again as Porsche and Volkswagen combine to create a mid-engine roadster/hardtop with contemporary performance at, hopefully, a reasonable price

Remembrances of things past do, in fact, obscure the bad and emphasize the good. How else does one account for the great affection Porsche fans hold for that teutonic version of a Lotus 7, the Speedster—a drafty, schizoid-handling tin can that spent nearly all of its time trying to trade ends and dedicated whatever was left over to rusting out. But since that model's death in late 1958, then the demise of the entire 356 series in 1964, and the subsequent leap in price of the 912/911 series, the American market in particular has been clamoring for another Speedster-type car from Stuttgart. Finally Porsche has decided to, at least partially, answer these demands, but rather than a roadster version of the 912/911 chassis a whole new car has been developed and comes in two versions, the 914 or the 914/6 (the "6" denoting a flat-six Porsche engine while the 914 is equipped with the flat-four from the VW 411—not, as one might assume, the old Porsche Four).

Even the most ardent admirers of the Speedster will admit that it was far from being a styling *tour de force* and if nothing else, the 914 carries on that tradition. But whereas the original Speedster was bulbous the new version has the fluidity of line of an Erector set project. The all-steel unit body incorporates a Targa-like integral rollbar to aid in structural rigidity for the coupe/hardtop 914. The single biggest disadvantage with this type of construction is the weight penalty Porsche has been forced to accept—the 85-hp 914 weighs 1984 lbs, while the 125-hp 914/6 is 2072 lbs.

If Corvette is looking for an argument to join the Lotus Europa and, now, the two newest Porsche models as the world's only production mid-engined cars, one need only to compare luggage space. The current front-engined Corvette has virtually none, for all of its 98-in. wheelbase and 182.5-in. length, while in the smaller 914s (96.5-in. wheelbase and overall length of 157 in.)

there is a full-sized trunk in front of the driver and a fitted storage rack for the removable steel hardtop over the transaxle.

Front suspension is by the now-standard-for-Porsche, MacPherson struts and longitudinal torsion bars. The rear, despite the fact that the transaxle is now mounted behind the engine, is also fairly standard Porsche theory with double-jointed halfshafts, trailing arms and coil springs. Because of the mid-engine location the extreme weight distribution that has long been a problem at Porsche almost ceases to exist and both 914s are not so prone to oversteer. A bonus is an accompanying improvement in ride quality. On both versions 4-wheel disc brakes are standard with the 914 utilizing 11.05-in. discs front, and 11.1-in. rear, while the more powerful 914/6 employs 11.12-in. vented front discs and 11.25-in. rears. The more powerful model also comes with 1-inch wider wheels.

As is befitting the $1700 price differential (in Germany where the pre-revaluation cost of the 914 was $3015 while the 914/6 sold for $4775) the interior as well as the engine compartment of the 914/6 is much less spartan than the 914. Both are strictly 2-seaters with only the driver's seat adjustable (the passenger is treated to an adjustable footrest). However, more lavish trim materials and convenient fingertip lights/wipers/horn stalks for the 914/6 immediately identify it as the top model in the series. Exterior identification clues as to which model is which are provided by the 914/6's vinyl covered rollbar, chromed bumpers and additional chrome trim molding (although social climbers can order the same stuff as options on the 914).

The VW 411 powerplant has been somewhat modified prior to the introduction of the Porsche 914, and performance with the 4-cylinder 1679cc, fuel-injected engine is about comparable with an MGB, with 0-60 mph times of 13.0 seconds and a top speed of 110 mph. Naturally, the 914/6 with the 6-cylinder 125-hp, twin 3-bbl. carbureted Porsche 911T engine, offers significantly better performance. Top speed for this model is over 120 mph with 0-60 being accomplished in just under 10 seconds. In addition, the 6-cylinder version offers much more mid-range torque which makes it a more pleasurable package all around, particularly for driving conditions in the United States. A 5-speed transmission is standard for both cars, although the 914/6 also offers the option of Porsche's semi-automatic "Sportomatic" transmission.—*David Phipps*

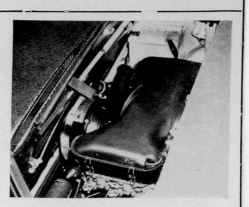

PORSCHE 914 (914/6)

VEHICLE TYPE
Mid-engined, rear-wheel-drive, 2-passenger sports car

ENGINE
Type: air-cooled, flat four (flat six), alloy block and heads
Bore x stroke..... 3.54 x 2.59 (3.14 x 2.59) in
Displacement................102 (221.5) cu in
Compression ratio.........8.2 (8.6) to one
Carburetion.........fuel injection (2 x 3-bbl)
Valve gear . Pushrod operated overhead valves
Power....................85 bhp @ 4900 rpm
(125 bhp @ 5800 rpm)
Torque................. 87 lb-ft @ 2800 rpm
(116 lb-ft @ 4200 rpm)

DRIVETRAIN
Transmission.................5-speed manual
Final drive ratio....................4.42 to one

SUSPENSION
F: Ind., MacPherson strut, torsion bars
R: Ind., trailing arms, coil springs

BRAKES
F:.........11.05-in disc (11.12-in vented disc)
R:...............11.10-in disc (11.25-in disc)

WHEELS AND TIRES
Wheel size.................4.5 x 15 (5.5 x 15)
Tire size and type.........155-SR 15 tubeless
(165-HR 15, tube type)

STEERING
Type......................Rack and pinion
Turning circle............................36.1 ft

DIMENSIONS AND CAPACITIES
Wheelbase..............................96.5 in
Track........F: 52.6 (53.6); R: 54.1 (54.4) in
Length....................................156.9 in
Width......................................64.9 in
Height............................48.0 (48.4) in
Curb weight.............1984 (2072) lbs
Fuel capacity.............................16.4 gal
Oil capacity.........................3.7 (8.5) qt

PERFORMANCE
0-60..................13.0 (9.9) seconds
Top speed...................110 (125) mph
*Performance figures for cars sold in the United States may vary due to installation of mandatory anti-smog equipment.

Porsche Power

BY STEPHAN WILKINSON

It comes in all sizes, from a gentle 86 horsepower to a turbocharged 234.

• Don't ask me why I had two at once, but in a day when I barely could afford one, I owned a pair of Porsches—two refrigerator-white 1956 Speedsters. One was a Carrera, a 1500 that was rumored (weren't they all?) to be "an ex-factory car." It was the GT model, which supposedly meant it had an aluminum hood and doors. The way I guarded that rare metal with constant warnings to passengers to close their door *very* gently and nightmares of sidewalk leaners crushing it like so much Reynolds wrap, you'd have thought it was Kryptonite.

Cams were the big deal in those days. Jaguars, Ferraris and Maseratis had two. So did Astons and Alfas, but nobody else of note had more than one. The Carrera had four. I was the only kid on my block who was able to say I had a quadruple-overhead-cam engine. It wasn't true, because all there was under the Speedster's little bustle was two horizontally opposed dohc banks—a VW

that got heads—but that little sucker added up to four, and nobody was going to convince me otherwise. It didn't matter that my Carrera went down the road crabwise, the unfortunate effect of the previous owner having slow-rolled it over a guard rail. I was still the only guy around with four cams.

Twenty years separate those old Speedsters (the other one was a 1600 Normal, little more than an arrogant Volkswagen) from their 1976 equivalents—the brand-new Turbo Carrera and the gently resurrected, VW-engined 912E. Yet the similarities between the '56 and '76 cars are far greater than the two-decade gap might suggest. My little Carrera was simply a street car with a 550 Spyder engine; the 1976 Turbo Carrera is just as straightforward a mating of race-car motor with civilized amenities. And just as the whole Speedster concept was an attempt to produce a People's Porsche, the 912E with its

four-cylinder VW engine hiding meekly under a 911's hemline is today's version of my old 60-horsepower 1600, a car that couldn't cover a Karmann Ghia.

The guiding principles still work as well as they ever did. The Turbo Carrera is a Panzer among Porsches, a street racer that will guarantee you a place at the top of the pecking order in a way that not even a Ferrari or a Lamborghini can, while the 912E is a domesticated quasi-Porsche perfect for the driver who can afford only half a loaf of sheer performance but wants a full helping of quality, prestige and operating economy.

The Turbo Carrera is a surprisingly modest car—almost too much so. There is little blatant visual drama beyond the classic Porsche shape, the now-familiar whale-tail spoiler and the compound curves of its wildly flared flanks. In fact, the squat, low-profile tires and diminutive size of the whole car make it look from some angles like a huge Dinky toy.

You'd expect louvers, vents, gauges and toggles for $26,000, but your doorman will think you bought a 911 with fender flares and a 180-mph speedometer. Not even a manifold-pressure gauge. A boost indicator would fit right where the clock goes in the present panel, and it would be a trick thing to have even though the turbo system operates automatically. After all, it wouldn't be any less functional than the car's electrically operated outside mirror.

We used to talk grandly of "getting on the cam," which was supposed to make it obvious that your engine had a peaky, high-performance torque curve. But the age of the turbo will change all that. From now on, you'll be "building boost." When you get the Turbo Carrera off the line and put your foot down hard, noth-

er during maximum-effort takeoffs when chassis/powertrain torque binds the linkage bushings and hangs up the lever momentarily between gears.

Though a five-speed gearbox with a lower first and closer-spaced gears would marginally decrease ET and allow you to spin the fat Pirelli CN36s almost at will (which is probably why the factory didn't provide it), the car is quite happy hustling along with four gears. It has mountains of torque, so the Turbo is a tremendously tractable car—as easy a high-performance machine to drive as any in the world. The interior is remarkably free of engine noise, with the turbocharger serving as a solid little energy- and sound-absorber; the steering is light at all speeds; and the pressure on the big clutch is not obtrusive.

Yet it's not a particularly *comfortable* car. Like those original four-cam Carreras, this is a Spyder for the street, not a "let's throw the Vuittons in the boot and dash to Biarritz, darling" grand tourer. The tires are harsh and suspension taut, and a series of prominent expansion strips can have you dodging around looking for the low spots. There's a considerable amount of wind and road noise, which is true of the 912E as well. A nice place to visit, but you wouldn't want to live there. Not that Porsche hasn't tried to furnish it grandly; the Turbo Carrera comes standard with a full leather interior, air conditioning, AM/FM, carpeting with "turbo" spelled out on the package deck behind the front seats—better there than in foot-high script on the sides of the car—and an automatic

> **6** The Turbo Carrera is a Panzer among Porsches, a street racer that will guarantee you a place at the top of the pecking order. **9**

ing surprising happens. The car accelerates almost lethargically, just like any 2800-pound, 3.0-liter, low-compression machine should. But when the rpms reach about 3000, an incredible slingshot suddenly launches the car. No production machine ever got on a cam as spectacularly as a turbocharged Porsche Carrera when its blower has spun up enough to poke its power through the intake ports.

This artificial aspiration is good for 13.5-second quarter-mile times and 103 mph through the trap, which are production-car figures you haven't seen much of since the late 1960s. You won't get any help from the Turbo Carrera's four-speed gearbox, though, for first is high enough to take you all the way to 51 mph; third and fourth are *both* overdrive ratios. If you can't keep the tires spinning, the revs at 3000 or 4000 off the line and the blower pumped up, the car will bog down long enough to add at least a second to your elapsed time. And if you're ever going to lose your grace under pressure, you'll do it with a Porsche's gearbox. What seems a precise transmission even under brisk road driving becomes a recalcitrant graunch-

Turbo's fenders are even wider than the normal Carrera's, as are tires and track.

The only Turbo option is a sunroof; everything from air to leather comes standard.

heater-control thermostat that retains the manual between-the-seats heat lever of the 911/912 but moves it electrically, as ponderously and mysteriously as one of those nonsense boxes where the hand comes out of the trap door and shuts off the switch. In fact, the only option available is a sunroof.

Yet the Turbo's task is not simply to be "tractable" or "comfortable" but to move on down the road. Which it does. At an indicated 158 mph (another *C/D* tester saw 160 during one run at the Ohio Transportation Research Center track), the car seems as docile as any other car at half that speed. It exhibits none of the twitchiness and front-end lightness that afflicts 911s at high speeds or in crosswinds. The car has extremely effective spoilers at both ends,

and they help the tires maintain their vertical load at high speeds. The Turbo also carries several suspension changes adapted directly from the company's racers: The front-end geometry comes straight from the Turbo RSR (the winged coupes campaigned in Europe by the Martini team), and the Turbo's angled rear trailing arms are of a new cast-aluminum shape known around the factory as "the banana," with geometry adapted from the 2.8 RSR.

One of the problems inherent in the standard Porsche's rear-suspension design is something called "deflection steer," which means that due to flexing of the fabricated steel trailing arm as well as the rubber bushings where the trailing arm is attached to the chassis, the rear wheels don't stay exactly paral-

lel to the centerline of the car. You can imagine what this does to a Porsche's desire to follow a straight path. The Turbo's new trailing-arm design, however, has decreased considerably any tendency toward deflection steer, and the extremely wide track and fat tires doubtless help as well.

The Turbo Carrera has a surprising amount of low-speed understeer—more so than even the standard 911. This is to some extent a designed-in trait, for if the car were much closer to neutral at low speeds, its oversteering tendencies at high speeds would be unmanageable.

Porsche handling is a subject of much contention, for the car has long defined "excellent handling" for many enthusiasts. So to hint otherwise is considered sacrilege. The truth is that what many of

Back by popular demand—and marketing strategy—the 912 had gone away in 1970.

The 912E's full interior and 2+2 seating are a prime advantage over the 914.

> The little four-cylinder 912E is your prototypical *road* car— comfortable where the Carrera is harsh, rational where the Carrera is excessive.

these people are talking about might better be called "apparent handling"— the supple, well-balanced way in which a Porsche eats up the bumps and ripples and camber changes of twisty back roads at brisk speeds, the precise steering and overall responsiveness of the car. Probe the depths of a Porsche's *real* handling, however—which can only be done on a large skidpad or road with plenty of room for spins and no threat of traffic—and you'll fish up the other side of the coin. And it's a coin that any Porsche owner ought to cash in at least once before pushing the car into a corner too fast. The difficulty (and fascination) of driving a Porsche truly hard is in trying to utilize handling that frequently and rapidly varies between the two extremes of insistent understeer and sudden oversteer. And to do so with a single corrective mode—power. Go into a corner too fast in a Porsche and you can't brake, back off or trust to the saving grace of understeer, because as soon as you lift, the rear end comes around in a classic illustration of what's called trailing-throttle oversteer. Porsches are sim-

(Text continued on page 74, specifications overleaf)

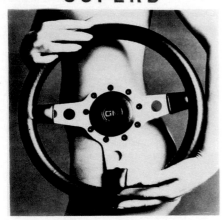

PORSCHE POWER

(Continued from page 45)

ply more stable under power than any other way.

On the track, the Turbo reveals itself as a rocket to be launched with extreme respect. The exhilaration of acceleration when the blower comes in is dangerously hypnotic, and there are corners of the car's performance envelope that are best left unexplored by any but the professionally skilled. Yet a race track is where this car is happiest, for it has such tremendous reserves of performance that nowhere else in this speed-limited land of ours will they ever be tapped.

The little four-cylinder Porsche 912E, on the other hand, is your prototypical *road* car. Leaping into and driving the 86-horsepower 912 after thundering around in the Turbo Carrera is not nearly so disappointing an experience as one might imagine. The 912 is comfortable where the Carrera is harsh, rational where the Carrera is excessive.

The 912E is the back-by-popular-demand reappearance of an honest little car that was introduced in 1966 and discontinued four years later: a 911-series body, chassis and interior mated to a docile 1.6-liter VW engine that could trace its own lineage all the way back to the mid-1950s. When the VolksPorsche 914 came along in 1970 with the same engine, the marketing men assumed that it would attract the attention of everybody who might otherwise have bought a 912. They missed the salient fact that the 914 is a two-seater of the starkest sort, and that the "full" Porsche accommodations of the 912 was one of its most attractive features. (Another reason for the early discontinuance of the 912 was that the car needed more power, and the old Porsche principle of overcarburetion to achieve that end was spiked by the onset of emissions regulations in the late 1960s. The 914 eventually got two liters and fuel injection, and that's what the 912E has today.)

To say the 912E is "satisfactory" is not praise as faint as it might at first sound. The little VW-engined car is satisfactory in so many ways that it all adds up to . . . well, certainly not a bargain but at least a grand alternative to a number of other cars that offer certain qualities at the expense of others. The 912E gets the job done: It accelerates briskly, goes fast, brakes well, eats gas as sparingly as any econobox, offers excellent quality and a comfortable interior, and above all gives you a satisfying feeling of being so

sensible. It's the kind of car that produces warm fantasies of an ordered world full of 912s, everybody decreed to drive these chugging little gumdrops, bustling about with great dispatch and economy and . . . *rationality.*

Remember, though, there's a big difference between being excited and being satisfied, and there's little exciting about the 912E. After all, half the excitement of a full-size Porsche is the sheer power. (If you still want that kick but can't afford the Turbo—of which Porsche only plans to import 400 in any case—there's still the standard six-cylinder 911S for 1976, though the Turbo has superseded the naturally aspirated Carrera model.)

On the skidpad, the 912 is a lot less comfortable to drive than the Turbo. It has considerably less roll stiffness, so the inside front wheel gets well off the ground as the body leans. (Unfortunately, Porsches don't have a dead pedal for a driver to brace against during hard cornering and braking—a surprising omission in so driver-oriented a car—and a few laps on the skidpad in either the Turbo or the 912E leave you feeling slightly clubfooted from trying to pretzel your left foot firmly onto the sloping sidewall or around the clutch pedal and onto the floorboard.)

Braking is one of the car's most mannerly maneuvers. The 912E stops straight and almost level—there's hardly any nose dip at all—and the front/rear proportioning is perfect. This is not so much an engineering feat as an inevitable result of the car's rearward weight bias, which tends to distribute the load evenly on all four wheels with forward weight transfer under braking.

In a world with no lack of $40,000 and $60,000 exoticars of the most extreme sort, the Turbo Carrera shows what practical design, constant refinement and assiduous development can accomplish. It has only six cylinders, the basic design is a good 12 years old, the headlights don't retract and your neighbors will never know it, but the Turbo Carrera is truly today's boss car. Drive it and there isn't *anybody* who's going to get there before you in a store-bought automobile.

And at the other end of the Porsche performance spectrum, there's the 912E—a car so sensible yet enjoyable that you begin to wonder whether Turbo Carreras are necessary at all. •

PORSCHE 912E

Importer: Porsche-Audi Division
Volkswagen of America, Inc.
Englewood Cliffs, NJ 07632

Vehicle type: rear-engine, rear-wheel-drive, 2 passenger coupe

Price as tested: $11,615.00
(Manufacturer's suggested retail price, including all options listed below, dealer preparation and delivery charges, does not include state and local taxes, license or freight charges)

Options on test car: base Porsche 912E, $10,845; forged alloy wheels, $495; AM/FM stereo radio, $200; dealer preparation, $75

ENGINE

Type:	flat-4, air-cooled, aluminum block and heads, cast iron cylinders, 3 main bearings
Bore x stroke	3.70x2.80 in, 94.0 x 71.1 mm
Displacement	120 cu in, 1971cc
Compression ratio	7.6 to one
Carburetion	Bosch L-Jetronic fuel injection
Valve gear	pushrod-operated overhead valves, solid lifters
Power (SAE net)	86 bhp @ 4900 rpm
Torque (SAE net)	93 lbs-ft @ 4000 rpm
Specific power output	0.72 bhp/cu in, 43.6 bhp/liter
Max. recommended engine speed	5600 rpm

DRIVE TRAIN

Transmission ....5-speed, all-synchro
Final drive ratio ....4.42 to one

Gear	Ratio	Mph/1000 rpm	Max. test speed
I	3.18	5.2	29 mph (5600 rpm)
II	1.83	9.0	51 mph (5600 rpm)
III	1.26	13.2	74 mph (5600 rpm)
IV	0.96	17.3	97 mph (5600 rpm)
V	0.72	23.0	111 mph (4850 rpm)

DIMENSIONS AND CAPACITIES

Wheelbase	89.4 in
Track, F/R	53.5/52.4 in
Length	168.9 in
Width	63.4 in
Height	52.8 in
Ground clearance	5.5 in
Curb weight	2455 lbs
Weight distribution, F/R	40.7/59.3 %
Battery capacity	12 volts, 44 amp-hr
Fuel capacity	21.1 gal
Oil capacity	3.7 qts

SUSPENSION

F: ....ind, MacPherson strut, torsion bars, anti-sway bar
R: ....ind, semi-trailing arm, torsion bars

STEERING

Type	rack and pinion
Turns lock-to-lock	3.1
Turning circle curb-to-curb	34.0 ft

BRAKES

F: ....11.1-in solid disc
R: ....11.4-in. solid disc

WHEELS AND TIRES

Wheel size	5.5 x 14 -in
Wheel type	forged aluminum, 5-bolt
Tire make and size	Uniroyal Rallye 240, 185HR-14
Tire type	steel belted radial ply, tubeless
Test inflation pressures, F/R	29/34 psi

PERFORMANCE

Zero to	Seconds
30 mph	3.0
40 mph	4.6
50 mph	6.7
60 mph	9.7
70 mph	13.6
80 mph	20.2
Standing ¼-mile	17.4 sec @ 76.4 mph
Top speed (observed)	111 mph
70-0 mph	204 ft (0.80 G)
Fuel economy, C/D mileage cycle	23.0 mpg, urban driving
	28.5 mpg, highway driving

The Turbo Carrera: Where All That Power Comes From

BY PATRICK BEDARD

It's not magic—just superior engineering.

• The Turbo Carrera's supercharging system is exactly what you'd expect of Porsche: complex, sophisticated and extremely effective. At low speeds, the only difference a driver would notice between the normally-aspirated 2.7-liter 911 and the 3.0-liter Turbo is a very slight lag in the Turbo's throttle response. From a standing start, the Turbo feels pretty much like any other 911, although you are aware of the long first gear ratio. Only difference is that the Turbo's power seems to double in the 500-rpm span between 2700 and 3200. This is accompanied by a hissing roar from the tailpipe as the volume of exhaust gases increases in proportion to the power. The traditional Porsche exhaust note is gone: Each cylinder's pulse is pureed by the turbine and comes out an acoustic applesauce.

Under full boost, the Turbo has the feel of a much larger engine. In contrast to the peaky 911S engines of days gone by, the Turbo's torque curve is dead level in the 4000/5000 rpm range and then drops gradually to the 6700 redline. There is a fair amount of turbo lag, however. When you move the throttle from its cruise position to wide-open, the engine is effectively naturally aspirated for a fraction of a second before the turbine can accelerate to its full-boost speed of

90,000 rpm. The lag is probably the result of the very long intake and exhaust passages inevitable with an opposed engine in a tightly packaged space. The exhaust gases are routed forward from each cylinder head through heat exchangers for the heater, then collected together and piped back along the left side of the engine through the waste gate and into the turbocharger at the left rear corner. The intake charge passes through an equally tortuous path. From an air cleaner on top of the engine it goes through the metering valve for the K-Jetronic fuel-injection system, then down to the left rear corner through the compressor, and finally back up on top of the engine, through the throttle valve and into the intake manifold.

The long distances don't really hurt anything once the boost is built up, but the transitions definitely suffer. Once you open the throttle, it takes a fair amount of time before the extra intake charge you've just admitted can burn, pass through all of the exhaust system and add its energy to the turbine wheel. And once the compressor starts to spin up, it still has a very long column of intake air to pressurize before the cylinders feel the effect. That's what makes turbo lag.

(Continued on page 75)

ACCELERATION standing ¼ mile, seconds

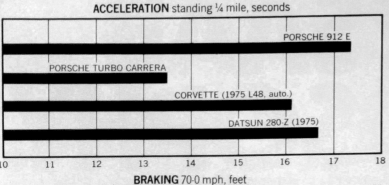

PORSCHE 912 E
PORSCHE TURBO CARRERA
CORVETTE (1975 L48, auto.)
DATSUN 280-Z (1975)

10 11 12 13 14 15 16 17 18

BRAKING 70-0 mph, feet

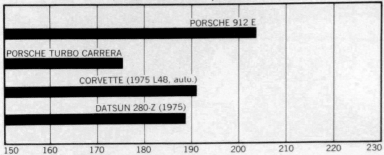

PORSCHE 912 E
PORSCHE TURBO CARRERA
CORVETTE (1975 L48, auto.)
DATSUN 280-Z (1975)

150 160 170 180 190 200 210 220 230

Tested by Automotive Environmental Systems, Inc.

FUEL ECONOMY C/D mileage cycle, mpg

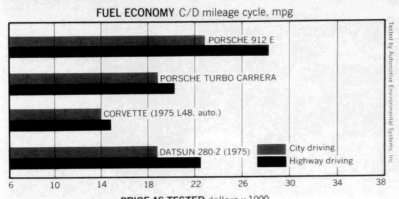

PORSCHE 912 E
PORSCHE TURBO CARRERA
CORVETTE (1975 L48, auto.)
DATSUN 280-Z (1975)

■ City driving
■ Highway driving

6 10 14 18 22 26 30 34 38

PRICE AS TESTED dollars x 1000

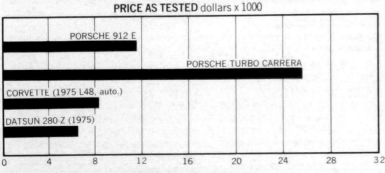

PORSCHE 912 E
PORSCHE TURBO CARRERA
CORVETTE (1975 L48, auto.)
DATSUN 280-Z (1975)

0 4 8 12 16 20 24 28 32

INTERIOR SOUND LEVEL dBA

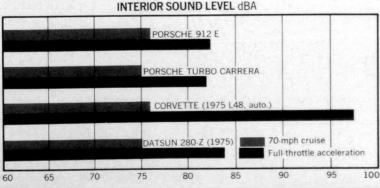

PORSCHE 912 E
PORSCHE TURBO CARRERA
CORVETTE (1975 L48, auto.)
DATSUN 280-Z (1975)

■ 70-mph cruise
■ Full-throttle acceleration

60 65 70 75 80 85 90 95 100

PORSCHE TURBO CARRERA

Importer: Porsche-Audi Division
Volkswagen of America, Inc.
Englewood Cliffs, NJ 07632

Vehicle type: rear-engine, rear-wheel-drive, 2 passenger coupe

Price as tested: $25,975.00
(Manufacturer's suggested retail price, including all options listed below, dealer preparation and delivery charges, does not include state and local taxes, license or freight charges)

Options on test car: base Porsche Turbo Carrera, $25,850; dealer preparation, $125

ENGINE
Type: flat-6 air-cooled, light alloy block and heads, 4 main bearings
Bore x stroke . . . . 3.74 x 2.77 in, 95.0 x 70.4 mm
Displacement . . . . 182.6 cu in, 2993cc
Compression ratio . . . . 6.5 to one
Carburetion . . . . Bosch CIS mechanical fuel injection
Valve gear . . . . chain-driven single overhead cam
Power (SAE net) . . . . 234 bhp @ 5500 rpm
Torque (SAE net) . . . . 246 lbs-ft @ 4500 rpm
Specific power output . . . . 1.28 bhp/cu in, 78.2 bhp/liter
Max. recommended engine speed . . . . 6700 rpm

DRIVE TRAIN
Transmission . . . . 4-speed, all-synchro
Final drive ratio . . . . 4.22 to one

Gear	Ratio	Mph/1000 rpm	Max. test speed
I	2.25	7.6	51 mph (6700 rpm)
II	1.30	13.2	88 mph (6700 rpm)
III	0.89	19.3	129 mph (6700 rpm)
IV	0.66	26.0	156 mph (6000 rpm)

DIMENSIONS AND CAPACITIES
Wheelbase . . . . 89.4 in
Track, F/R . . . . 56.4/59.1 in
Length . . . . 168.9 in
Width . . . . 69.9 in
Height . . . . 52.0 in
Ground clearance . . . . 5.9 in
Curb weight . . . . 2825 lbs
Weight distribution, F/R . . . . 36.5/63.5 %
Battery capacity . . . . 12 volts, 66 amp-hr
Fuel capacity . . . . 21.1 gal
Oil capacity . . . . 11.6 qts

SUSPENSION
F: . . . . ind, MacPherson strut, torsion bars, anti-sway bar
R: . . . . ind, semi-trailing arm, torsion bars, anti-sway bar

STEERING
Type . . . . rack and pinion
Turns lock-to-lock 3.1
Turning circle curb-to-curb . . . . 35.1 ft

BRAKES
F: . . . . 11.2-in. dia vented disc
R: . . . . 11.4-in. dia vented disc

WHEELS AND TIRES
Wheel size . . . . F: 7.0 x 15-in; R: 8.0 x 15-in
Wheel type . . . . forged aluminum alloy, 5-bolt
Tire make and size . . . . Pirelli Cinturato CN36, F: 185/70 VR-15
R: 215/60 VR-15
Tire type . . . . steel belted radial, tube type
Test inflation pressures, F/R . . . . 28/33 psi

PERFORMANCE
Zero to   Seconds
    30 mph 1.9
    40 mph 2.7
    50 mph 3.7
    60 mph 4.9
    70 mph 6.3
    80 mph 7.9
    90 mph 10.2
    100 mph 12.9
Standing ¼-mile . . . . 13.5 sec @ 102.6 mph
Top speed (observed) . . . . 156 mph
70-0 mph . . . . 176 ft (0.93 G)
Fuel economy, C/D mileage cycle . . . . 19.0 mpg, urban driving
20.5 mpg, highway driving

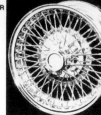

TURBO CARRERA

(Continued from page 46)

Porsche engineers have taken some elaborate steps to compensate, howev-er. First, they've chosen a turbocharger with a tight exhaust scroll (the tighter the scroll, the higher the turbine speed with any given exhaust flow). This allows compressor speed to build rapidly. Then to prevent overboosting, they've provid-ed a waste gate to bypass exhaust around the turbine when the desired in-take manifold pressure—in this case 11.4 psi—is reached. So the system reaches full boost by about 3000 rpm, which results in the commendably flat torque curve.

Porsche engineers have also made an elaborate attempt to maintain high com-pressor speed in those situations where the driver momentarily lifts off the throt-tle and then gets back on the power again. To do this, another bypass valve has been incorporated in the system be-tween the compressor outlet and the throttle valve. When the throttle is closed, the bypass valve opens to recir-culate compressor outlet pressure back around to the compressor inlet. This al-lows the compressor turbine to operate in what approaches a no-load situation; therefore turbine speed decays slowly. A conventional system would have the compressor coast down against the full restriction of the closed throttle, and speed would be rapidly lost.

All of this elaborate machinery oper-ates automatically, and even the worst possibilities have been anticipated. Waste gates are notoriously unreliable; they are inclined to stick closed and over-boost the engine. The Turbo Carrera has a pressure switch in the intake manifold that shuts off the fuel if the boost ex-ceeds 16 psi, so the engine is not likely to blow itself up. And there is an ignition interrupter set for the redline to keep the driver from getting carried away. About the only way to sabotage the works is a tank of low-octane gasoline, which could result in detonation and piston failure. Porsche specifies a minimum of 96 oc-tane.

Naturally, any powerplant this compli-cated will have its service problems. The car we tested had a bad case of the low-speed jerks, which has so far defied di-agnosis. It's apparently not typical, be-cause we had previously driven another car that behaved perfectly.

And believe us, when a Turbo Carrera is right, it's really right.

CAR and DRIVER

APRIL 1978

SUPERTEST:

PORSCHE

928 and 930

BY DON SHERMAN

*They defy comparison,
but as Ultimate Porsches they're the standards
by which all future sports cars
will be judged.*

Continued

Porsches have always been exclusive. The 928 and the 930 carry on that tradition. Their price, performance and personality insure that only those with well-tempered palates, well-stuffed wallets and above average skills buy and keep them. The arrangement is the price of a search for perfection.

Continued

928: *The driver's car reinvented*

• The baton is officially passed. Porsche has a magnificent new runner to carry its prestige, the 928. After 30 years of compulsive rear-engine development, the firm's technical brilliance has been redirected to a new generation of front engine/rear transmission cars.

The transition bodes well, even though not a single 928 is yet in the hands of a U.S. owner. This new Porsche generated rave introductory reviews a year ago, and European magazine editors wasted no time heralding it their 1978 Car of the Year. Now that American test cars have passed through our scrutiny, we can add our applause. The 928 is as good as it is different, and it's a whole lot different than any Porsche that's gone before.

The only tradition saved for the 928 is the dauntless quest for distinction. This is manifested by the styling, which is purposely controversial. During two weeks of testing the first 928 released on the street, it was systematically exposed to several critics with widely varying responses. One immediately pronounced it ugly, but most people found it intriguing, although too much like an inflated 924. Not a soul was bold enough to endorse the 928, bug-eyes and all, as a thing of beauty on first sight. These responses also seem typical of hundreds of southern California highway encounters, where we found that the new Porsche is definitely *not* a head turner. The masses ignore it. Part of the problem is the ultra low-key identification—the Porsche crest appears only in the traditional center-hood spot, and the seven sacred letters but once in relief across the tail section. For no apparent reason, the critical 928 digits are tucked away like military code. Only the most dedicated inspector will find them hidden along the lower run of flat-black rear window trim.

Porsche's philosophical shifts in the 928 are just as brazen as the styling. This is the biggest road Porsche ever—dimensionally the 928 is a 924 stretched by six inches in length and width—and two Porsche firsts come built in: a fairly serious attempt at a back seat and a real automatic transmission option. The bigness, roominess and comfort mean that the 928 isn't a Porsche sports car at all, but is instead shooting for the upper reaches of grand touring. This crucial shift may mean that out of the ranks of Porsche freaks, only mature 911 owners are likely to find contentment here. Perhaps guys who bought the soft-suspension experiment in 1977 will make the cut, but more than likely, the 928 will be the Porsche for those who never liked Porsches.

With this clean sheet of design paper and fresh list of potential clients, Porsche has bought itself a rare chance to impress just about every living soul with a speck of car consciousness. The opportunity has been well exploited in the 928, because it has something for everyone. The crown of fuel injection castings atop the engine will knock out the technical fetishists, the driving experience will fire the imaginations of both real and imagined racing impressarios and the comfort is knee-deep for the growing ranks of automotive voluptuaries. If this weren't enough, Porsche has made the 928 practical to maintain—another about-face—with hydraulic valve lifters, 15,000-mile oil change intervals and easy-to-reach spark plugs.

Everybody loves a broad-shouldered V-8, so just raising the hood wins a 928 convert every time. And while we've rumbled down the rocky road of progress with V-8s for decades, none has been so painstakingly designed as this. Running or still, inside the car or displayed on a pedestal, fully dressed in emissions controls or stripped to the bare block, the Porsche V-8 is functional aluminum sculpture. It has no racing aspirations, there are admitted cost cuts and the power curves are modest for a Porsche, but the new engine is by any standard a brilliant design.

Probably the ultimate compliment came from a Porsche freak we encountered in southern California. He knew all about the 928, had one on order and eagerly followed us to an appointment at the Briggs Cunningham museum. While Mr. Cunningham took his first drive in the 928, the very trendy Porschephile—black-designer sunglasses, regulation Gucci belt and loafers, meticulously tailored blue jeans and all—relished his first physical encounter with the new Porsche. After the initial round of gawking and poking was over, Briggs very deliberately adjusted the 928 to his build, keyed the noisy starter to life and motored off on his test run. The Porschephile was speechless for an instant and then finally let go with his pronouncement, "Gee, it sounds just like a Pontiac."

The fact of the matter is, the Porsche 928 engine has a lot more in common with the American Way than just the rumble of its exhaust. In rough terms, the Porsche V-8 is a double Vega engine. The block is a linerless aluminum die-casting and each bank of cylinders has one belt-driven cam actuating inline valves through hydraulic lifters. Piston displacement is 4474cc, also roughly twice what Chevrolet gave us in the Vega. From this point on, the thinking is uniquely Porsche with innovations like

Continued

SUPERTEST *Continued*

sintered steel powder connecting rods (stronger, lighter and cheaper than a forged part) and the world's first single belt drive for a production overhead-cam V-8.

Superior technology and all, the Porsche engine feels little more exciting than a good American V-8 with an extra 1000 revs on the tach. Both torque and horsepower ratings are in fact very close to the Corvette L-82. The long tuned intake passages and mild cam timing skew the torque curve toward the low rpm side, so you can engage the clutch at idle, flatten the gas pedal and motor away as smoothly as a Cadillac. What you lose is the rev-forever arrogance of a 911. The 928 motor does its best work strongly and quietly well below the 5250rpm horsepower peak.

This may sound like a pretty dull fate for the Porsche of the Eighties, at least until you realize just how strong the 928 is while it's being quiet. One bright winter day we cranked off a top-speed run of 144 mph. It takes miles to wind up the 170 mph speedometer even after you're in fifth, but the 928 doesn't level out until almost all the available revs are present and accounted for. Minutes later we blasted down the drag strip. With a 0-60 time of 6.4 seconds and quarter-mile results of 15.3 seconds at 92.6 mph, the 928 does pretty well for a car developed in the depths of the energy crisis. Only something imported that says "Porsche" on the hood will touch it and the only domestics within sniffing distance are Pontiac's Trans Am and the L-82 Corvette. Fifth gear handles those two nicely.

The one design feature that outranks the engine in both subtlety and influence is the chassis layout. The seven-foot breach between the engine and transmission affects road holding, ride, interior roominess and even throttle response. Placing the 928's masses at the extreme ends of the wheelbase achieves the design intent of a high polar moment of inertia, which in simple terms means the flywheel effect of the car is maximized in both horizontal and vertical planes. Transient response to any steering input is therefore slower. The body also has a high resistance to pitching on wavy pavement, and upon hard throttle or brake applications. The high polar-moment design makes the 928 feel more deliberate in its movements than either the 3420-pound curb weight or any past Porsche layout might initially suggest.

There are other lesser effects from this configuration. Back-seat room suffers from driveline and transmission intrusion. The four-foot long, 0.98-inch diameter drive

shaft twists significantly when force to deliver the engine's full 254 foot-pounds of torque, and this occasionally filters back through the driveline as surging in the lower gears. Three factors—slight lunging when you overindulge the throttle around town, the long and imprecise engagement of the two-plate clutch and the unpopular "racing" shift pattern of the five-speed transmission—could well justify serious consideration of the no-cost automatic transmission option.

With or without a clutch, a Porsche would not be a Porsche without distinguished handling, so we were most anxious to investigate this latest word from the Weissach test track. Since the heavens opened up with a solid week of rain the instant we laid hands on our California test car's keys, there was ample opportunity to analyze wet pavement manners in the 928. The Pirelli P7 radials don't look like much of a rain tire but they don't act like they look. On a wet skidpad complete with standing puddles, we cranked off easy 0.75 g laps and tried everything you shouldn't try on slick pavement—stomping on the gas, mashing the brakes and rudely wrenching the steering wheel, none of which was enough to crack the 928's composure. You can slide all four wheels on this car, pitch it 60 degrees sideways and it comes back every time. Recovery is easier than parallel parking: lift off the gas, let the power steering re-center the wheel and you're straight.

The dry skidpad was just as thrilling. Here the P7s get down to serious race tire behavior: They stick like epoxy right up to 0.80 g. Understeer prevails unless you step into the throttle and the tail then moves out as if your right foot ran a rear wheel steering system. This is because it does. The patented Weissach rear axle is highly touted for its lift-throttle *understeer* contribution (retarding forces at the tire on overrun or braking deflect the compound trailing-link bushings in such a way that the rear wheels toe in slightly). But the reverse effect is also present: stepping into the throttle steers the rear tires out. This tendency, along with the 928's high polar moment of inertia, makes the tail much more responsive to the throttle than it is to the steering wheel—just the reverse of the 911 series. So you steer the front with your hands and the back with your right foot and, using both, the 928 will do just about whatever you please.

The only problem is, you'll likely never see a 928 flung about like the big sports car its chassis knows it is. There are just too many soothing influences that suggest this

Continued

is a Porsche to be savored rather than spurred. For example, the ride insists that the 928 is a luxury car. The high polar moment seems to repave wavy asphalt as you go, and the tires are downright plush in their way with bumps, even though each one carries 36 pounds of air. There's also noticeable longitudinal compliance in the suspension, so hard tar strips just dissolve in the works. You may occasionally hear them, but anything you *feel* is a serious bump. What it adds up to is the finest combination of ride and handling ever bolted under one car roof.

The brakes are just as good, but it's hard to tell from the driver's seat. Ford, in the Fifties, used a lot of pro-dive geometry in its front suspensions to pitch the front bumper down to pavement level the instant you touched the brake pedal. The purpose was to make folks think they had terrific brakes when in fact they didn't. The reverse effect prevails in the 928: You can't tell you've just hooked anchor because there's absolutely no drama. The body stays flat and you don't wiggle or waver an

inch off course. If you keep pushing well past P7 tires' warning signs of imminent lockup, one rear wheel will slide, but there's still no loss of stability. So you'll have to take the 928's brakes on faith. The test results say you have nothing to worry about, as we recorded easily repeatable stops from 70 mph in a very short 182 feet.

Performance numbers have historically been the heart and soul of Porsches, and while the 928 has its own impressive set of cocktail credentials, you don't have to blast this car around at eleven-tenths to feel you've gotten your money's worth. And there are so many toys inside to play with that extra-legal speeds are never necessary to stave off boredom: an air-conditioned glove box, a sound system that will play everything but Radio Free Europe, twin electric mirrors, three separate window washers systems, and even a knob to adjust headlamp aim. Automatic speed control has at least found a car that really needs servo-assistance. Without it, fifth gear on metro freeways is an invitation to arrest, because an ounce of throttle pres-

928 chassis: Up front, a 4.5-liter V-8;
in the middle, a torque tube;
in back, the gearbox and Weissach axle.

sure will take you deep into forbidden speed ranges. With a near-total absence of wind or engine noise, you have the choice of staring at the speedometer or automatic cruising to make it through cop corridors.

Night riding brings out the finest tricks in the 928's interior. One click of the key lights up the full marquee of red indicators—seventeen in all—that at the appropriate time will warn you of everything but a receding hairline. The next click extinguishes the distress signals and energizes the six gauges directly concerned with getting you about your appointed rounds. The whole cluster adjusts with the steering wheel, so the built-in 911 problem of hidden needles is hereby solved with typical Porsche thoroughness. We would suggest one minor alteration. Unless Porsche has some future use in mind for the 170-mph speedometer, a 150-mph unit with wider markings would be easier to use.

Riders are just as well cared for in the 928 with a level of comfort downright decadent by old Porsche standards. There's a very carefully concealed light-up vanity mirror sure to make waves at Porsche Club meetings. The seats have what feel to be the softest cushions Recaro has ever supplied any manufacturer, although after you settle in, there is firm lateral restraint. The bold sweep of wrap-around console will certainly be appreciated long after initial thrills of dropping into the 928's twin jet cockpits have passed. It's a great way to locate vent registers and air flow close to your face for maximum effectiveness.

The only significant transgression Porsche interior designers will be charged with is failing their back seat trust. If you've somehow found enough room in the back of a Firebird, you'll be right at home here. Those who were hoping for a real four-seater Porsche will be disappointed. The 928 was conceived a 2+2 in 1971 and even energy-crisis second thoughts couldn't move this company out of seating. The back seats are well padded and comfy to sit on, but leg room is directly proportional to the front passengers' benevolence, and head room is marginal even with the rear sun visors deployed. At least the rear seat backs fold separately so you can pack luggage around one passenger if necessary.

The vision is not yet crystal-clear, but what you see here is the way things will be. Porsche alone has seized the initiative to reinvent the driver's car and the 928 is the most appealing look at the future yet revealed. It's already the best car we've ever tested. And in the hands of the world's most dedicated developers, the 928's potential is unlimited. ●

Super Turbo: *the people's racer*

• Now that Porsche's future is secure in a GT for the Eighties, the legendary Turbo has been called back to the labs. Result: Its torque curve has been packed with nitroglycerin and it's loose again like a mad dog on the streets. They call it Super Turbo, and only professional drivers with up-to-date medical certificates and fresh advanced training slips from the Bondurant school need apply. What we have here is the first volume-produced and perfectly legal car in America capable of tripling the national speed limit.

You must realize that Porsche most definitely did not set 165 mph as a design goal for the new Turbo. The engineers have better things to do than mocking our speed limits, as inane as they might be. But all this racing technology was lying around, and as the world's most dedicated practitioners of "speed improves the breed," the Zuffenhausen wizards followed their consciences as only they can by bolting it all into one super Porsche.

It's no secret the 911's days are numbered. Emissions and noise standards will eventually catch up to this throwback from the Thirties and purge America of all air-cooled Beetles and Porsches in one fell swoop. And the Turbo's existence also makes it obvious that Porsche isn't going to let that era end with a whimper. The

stoking-up for an unforgettable exit blaze of glory has already begun in the furnace below the Turbo's whale tail.

Just sitting here, flat on the page, it looks as ferocious as a beehive. The back end is swollen like the neck of an angry sumo wrestler. You can see "Porsche" cast on finned aluminum brake calipers through the wheel vents. Fat tires stick out at every corner. The rubber looks sticky enough to trap flies and there are these little aluminum braces for the valve stems. Could a car be so fast the valve stems can't cope? The answer has to be yes.

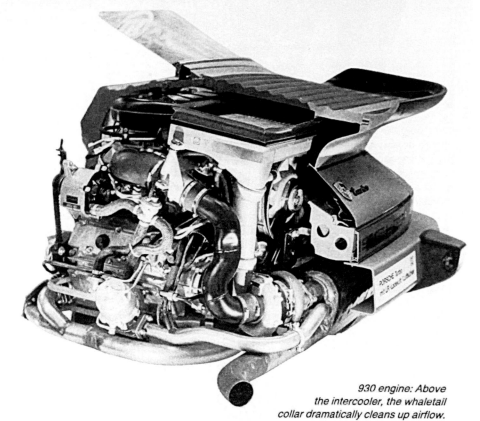

930 engine: Above the intercooler, the whaletail collar dramatically cleans up airflow.

Inside the Turbo is just a 911 that's been to all the right stores. Very nice-smelling leather on the instrument panel, steering wheel and seats, very natty cloth for the upholstery and door panels. The carpeting is almost thick enough to hide your loafers, but all this comfort is a ruse. The Porsche Turbo is in truth a full-throttle fiend, and the moment you get strapped in and start the motor, it won't quit until every last needle is off scale.

You know it's deadly when the thing idles as smooth as a Subaru. The exhaust is practically silent and the tail section is so packed with power pieces that the fan whir doesn't even get out. Who ever heard of a Porsche without a racket in back?

If you possess priestly restraint, you might go four miles in the Turbo before

Continued

SUPERTEST *Continued*

you stomp the gas pedal with both feet and let the mighty torque curve ratchet you back a few notches in the seat. Just be sure to keep one eye on the tach, your right hand on the gear shift and your white knuckles somewhere near the nine o'clock spot on the steering wheel. Opening the throttle wide is just like parking on railroad tracks. When the turbo comes on, the 5:15 to Hartford has just kissed your back bumper. But it doesn't last long. Yank the long lever twice and you'll see a 100 in twelve seconds. If you're good in traffic, you'll pull 130 in a mile. And if your driving record is shot anyway, go ahead, stay with it. Yes, the turbo will bury its 150 mph speedometer needle with a neat, clean ten percent extra for good measure.

To add these nine miles per hour to the 1977 Turbo's top speed, Porsche engineers have pretty well started over. That meant using the best parts from the old Turbo, the latest tricks from the race track and a multitude of new designs. And since the effort is spread over only 350 American customers, it's not hard to see why the Turbo's new price is $34,000 almost double that of the 911SC.

The 1978 engine is bigger at 3.3 liters and this necessitated all-new major components: crankcase, crankshaft, cylinders, pistons and connecting rods. The KKK turbocharger is also larger to feed the monster and an intercooler has been added after such an approach proved very effective on the racetrack.

With the turbo trying to force-feed the engine at a maximum pressure of 11.8 psi, intake air can be heated to 265 degrees Fahrenheit. This saps much of the turbocharger's contribution to higher efficiency. The solution is to cool the intake charge between the compressor and the intake manifold with a simple heat exchanger known as an air-to-air intercooler. This device looks like a conventional aluminum radiator with the intake charge routed inside and cool air flowing over outside surfaces. The supply of cooling air comes from the high pressure (top) side of the whale-tail spoiler and enters the engine compartment through slits. After it passes over the intercooler's tube and fin latticework, this same air is drawn to the engine cooling fan and circulated through normal flow passages. Having cooled first the intake charge and then the engine, the flow exhausts out the bottom.

For such a simple device, the intercooler's contribution is substantial. The Super Turbo motor has a net torque advantage of fifteen percent over the three-liter Turbo, ten percent of which comes from this year's added displacement and five percent from the new intercooler.

These 3.3 liters feel more like six because tight exhaust turbine passages start the boost just above idle. What's perceived as "lag" is not a lack of throttle response, but the time it takes the turbine to spin up. When it makes 90,000 rpm, you've got an extra 33 hp under your right foot. With the throttle wide open, you get three pounds of boost at 2000 rpm, eight pounds at 3000 rpm and the full 11.8 pound load just past 4000 rpm. This makes the torque peak a full 1000-rpm-wide plateau.

Wrapped around this miracle motor is a car that Porsche doesn't even consider a 911. The Turbo is known as the 930 be-

cause in addition to the engine, it has a unique transmission, clutch, front and rear suspension, brakes, tires and bodywork. The 930 is the ultimate road-going refinement of Dr. Porsche's original Volkswagen.

Nothing but the best is good enough for such a car, including tires. Pirelli Cinturato P7s are the world's finest performance tires and they've been used by Porsche for over a year. As worn by the Turbo, these tires are great for turning and stopping, but they're too sticky for smooth light-off from the rest. During acceleration testing we encountered terminal wheel tramp which made the Turbo feel like a sewing machine gone berserk trying to stitch itself into the pavement. All through first gear each rear tire left foot-long black smears, interrupted by two-foot gaps of clean pavement. This is the primary reason acceleration times haven't improved over the 1976 Turbo, even though quarter-mile speed is up by 1.6 mph. Zero-to-sixty has stabilized at 4.9 seconds.

Sticky tires, excellent rear wheel traction and the mastadon motor team up to create a genuine immovable object/irresistable force situation. To lash it all together, Porsche has specified a new higher-capacity clutch. The pressure plate is a heavy iron casting to smooth out torsional vibrations with more flywheel inertia. And the clutch disc now has a massive rubber hub to eliminate driveline noise caused by irregular torque pulses through the gearbox. The new assembly is so bulky the entire engine must be moved back 1.2 inches in the body to fit everything in.

More weight in the tail is of course the last thing the Turbo needs for handling, but it does pay off in braking. There is no car sold in America that stops better than this Porsche. In addition to 63.8 percent of the weight on the back tires, this car benefits from its P7 tires, a very sensitive vacuum booster and a set of brakes that worked just great in the 917 race car. Even if they didn't haul the Turbo down from 70 in 168 feet, you'd gladly pay extra for brakes that look as good as these. The rotors are cast with curved radial vents to produce maximum surface area and cross-drilled to optimize both heat rejection and wet performance. The calipers are beautiful finned-aluminum castings with four pistons per wheel. A proper bed-in procedure is apparently crucial, because we had to live with shrill brake squeal after our normal cycle of brutal stopping tests.

Handling is always a thorny subject when speaking of rear-engined Porsches. Like the fabulous Auto Union Grand Prix

Continued

racers of the Thirties, there are never-ending accounts of treacherous oversteer, many of which should be filed under "Old Wives Tales." The fact of the matter is, you don't *have* to be a Bernd Rosemeyer to drive the Turbo fast and hard when the road squiggles, but it helps.

We found that five minutes of skidpad testing this car is the exercise equivalent of 50 push ups. Staying on top of the Turbo's persistent swings between heavy understeer and tail-out oversteer requires sawing back and forth on the wheel. And steering that is normally light and quick on the street gets really heavy in twisting the sticky P7 tires through such large slip angles. Our test results show this car will corner at 0.81 g, but what you can actually use on the road is well below that figure.

Under/oversteer is just one of the many evil traits that must be wrestled into submission before you become the Turbo's master. Steep first-gear acceleration will jerk one wheel right off the ground if you light the booster exiting a slow turn. The shift linkage occasionally binds up during high-rpm gear changes to add a little extra excitement. And there are hidden aerodynamic curves built into the Porsche Turbo as well. Speed lightens front wheel loadings dramatically, so understeer goes up with velocity. This would be a marvelous safety device were it not for the Turbo's lift-throttle antics. Aerodynamic understeer tricks you into lifting off the throttle when the nose starts drifting wide in a high-speed turn. It's not the right thing to do, as Auto Union ace Rosemeyer probably knew, because this reverses longitudinal forces in the rear suspension. The back wheels toe out, the tail swings wide and your whole SCCA driving career flashes before your eyes. The Turbo won't spin easily, but things can get very scary if you don't hang in there with some throttle and lots of steering.

There is more stability this year with the new tall-collar whale tail that cuts rear lift by 70 percent over a clean decklid, and by twenty percent over the original design. Air flow to the engine is also improved, even though there is no increase in aerodynamic drag.

So what Dr. Ferdinand Porsche conceived as a 25-hp KdF-wagen 40 years ago has been turboed, intercooled, spoilered, P7ed and worked over so diligently that it has become the fastest volume-produced car in the world. It's not much of a people's car any more. In fact, most of those who can afford the Turbo would be wise to hang it on the wall like the valuable piece of auto-art it is. The rest of us can dream and maybe toss an occasional hunk of raw meat into the garage once in a while as if we actually had one.　●

PHOTOGRAPHY: HUMPHREY SUTTON

Continued
CAR and DRIVER

CAR and DRIVER
ROAD TEST

Porsche 944

The most seductive combination of economy and performance money can buy.

The Porsche 944 is a great car. It renews your faith in Porsche, because the men who made the 944 put into it everything they know about fast cars. It renews your faith in fast cars, fast living, and fast women, because it brings you these things at a reasonable price and with fuel efficiency besides. From now on, Porsche performance is no longer restricted to those entertainment lawyers in L.A. who scuttle through Coldwater Canyon in their 911s and 928s on their way from their homes in Studio City to their warrens in Century City. The rest of us can finally have a piece of the action.

Of course, all Porsches are supposed to be serious automobiles. But sometimes it's been hard to keep the faith. First there was the 914, with its Volkswagen engine. Then came the 924, with its Audi drivetrain. Neither car was intended to be a Porsche: the 914 was marketed as a VW-Porsche in Europe and the 924 was developed to be an Audi sports car. Finally, the succession of 924s equipped

with tape stripes and special equipment hasn't bolstered Porsche's reputation as a maker of serious cars, either.

With the 944, however, Porsche has at last made over the 924 in its own image. The forthcoming demise of the 924's economical but rough-running engine, shared with such lesser forms as the AMC Spirit and one VW truck, provided the opportunity. Even in 1976, when the 924 was introduced, Porsche engineers recognized the limitations of the 2.0-liter four-cylinder and developed two alternatives. One was a 3.5-liter, 90-degree V-6 derived from the 928 engine; but experimentation with a 2.8-liter V-6 developed by Peugeot, Renault, and Volvo revealed that such an engine would weigh too much, consume too much fuel, run roughly, and be difficult to install on the assembly line. So it proved to be the second alternative that is being built at Porsche and installed on Audi's 944 production line.

This all-aluminum, 2.5-liter in-line four-cylinder duplicates the 924 engine's weight and fuel economy, but produces 30 percent more power. Just as important, the 944 engine carries two Mitsubishi-style balance shafts to exorcise objectionable engine vibes. More anti-vibration science went into the engine's mounting arrangement as well. Special shock-absorbing mounts attach the engine to a new, vibration-resistant aluminum crossmember, and the crossmember itself is connected to the chassis at points that are relatively insensitive to vibration. Just to emphasize that this engine,

derived from the 928's V-8, is designed to do serious business, there's a Porsche logotype cast prominently into the valve cover.

The 944's cockpit environment has also been improved to eliminate the dentist-drill resonances that plagued the 924. First, the thick sound insulation developed for the 924 Turbo is carried over into the 944. The rack-and-pinion steering is mounted in rubber to improve isolation from road shocks, and the tie rods feature rubber bits for the same reason. Finally, a rubber-damped clutch and new transmission mounts keep the drivetrain from buzzing like a Swedish sexual appliance. Porsche's testing reveals that seat-of-the-pants vibes in the 944 are less severe than those of other sports cars (although it's unclear *which* sports cars), while engine noise is less than that of a conventional four-cylinder below 2500 rpm and equivalent to a smooth-running V-6 or V-8 above that mark.

As long as the guys in the lab coats at Weissach had the 924 laid out on the operating table, they decided to transplant some muscle into the chassis too. So the four-wheel disc brakes optional on the 924 Turbo are standard on the 944. The track has been increased 2.3 inches in front and 3.1 inches in back. Big 215/60VR-15 tires ride on cast wheels with seven-inch rims (205/55VR-16 tires on forged wheels with seven-inch rims are optional). Finally, weight distribution fore and aft is almost exactly equal and the suspension calibration falls midway between the 924 Turbo's and the European GTS Carrera's.

Wrapped around this package is the bodywork of the Euro Carrera, with its odd but powerful mixture of curves from the styling studio and angles from the racetrack. The 944 has a larger cross-sectional area than the 924, but a better drag coefficient (0.35, versus the 924's 0.36). A special windshield molding to reduce turbulence and a longer rear spoiler account for some of this improvement, but the major contribution comes from the elastic urethane nose, which routes air under the bumper and into the radiator very efficiently.

When you run all this stuff through your memory banks, of course, you realize that the 944 simply represents another brew of Porsche special equipment. Even the engine simply produces the same power as the 924 Turbo's. So why should this car be better? The point is, the 944 incorporates all of Porsche's *good* stuff. Porsche engineers built the 944 to be the kind of car that Porsche engineers like to drive.

PHOTOGRAPHY BY AARON KILEY

You can feel the dedication to speed simmering inside the 944 even when you're droning down the turnpike. The car lopes along at about the same rpm as the 924 Turbo—both cars are geared almost identically, with very tall fourth and fifth gears—and 62-mph cruising delivers over 30 mpg and tremendous range from the 16.4-gallon fuel tank. Yet, unlike any 924, this car feels calm and composed, almost like a 928. And when you stick your foot in it, the high-compression engine gets you rolling right away without downshifting.

To be sure, the cockpit is more intense on the freeway than your average Chevy Caprice, but the 944 feels like a water bed compared with a 924, simply because engine noise and vibration are imperceptible. And the new ventilation system, which routes fresh air to all ducts and features 928 pieces in the standard air conditioning, takes the edge off the heat transmitted by all that glass surrounding the cockpit. You'll still find yourself wincing over expansion joints, though. Porsche engineers admit that the Rabbit suspension in the front and the VW microbus suspension in the rear just don't provide large enough rubber bushings to build in much compliance without making the handling all rubbery as well. So even though new top bushings for the front MacPherson struts improve road isolation somewhat, you'd be well advised to avoid Third Avenue in Manhattan and the entire state of West Virginia.

But listen, you want to know what the 944 is like once you crank it up to warp speed, right? Well, it's terrific. You can drive like a hero without sweat popping out on your brow. The 944 is great because it responds crisply and decisively to every command, and it builds up to its limits in a perfectly linear fashion. You won't find killer understeer here. And you won't find any nervousness at the limit either. You will find yourself catching the rhythm of Ortega Highway or Angeles Crest or your local racer road like a hill-climb champion. Feel free to hunt 911s if you wish, because even though the 944 gives away 29 hp and 130 pounds to the superest Super Beetle, it can be driven at the limit effortlessly, while it takes some concentration to drive the 911 more than six corners in a row without making a mistake.

It's as if the 944 had been developed in long drives through the Alps, rather than in short sprints around Porsche's Weissach test track. The cockpit environment at speed is calm. You always feel as if you are traveling much slower than the new yellow numerals on the speedometer tell you—that is, if the needle hasn't run out of numerals to read altogether. The suspension soaks up each bump and then damps the ride motion immediately. The engine revs crisply, but there's more than 130 pounds-feet of torque between 2500 rpm and 5500 rpm, so there's not much need to seek redline. The brakes are plenty powerful, although there's too much boost (just as with every 924 since 1976) and the pedal rides a little high for really effortless heel-and-toe action. There's no need to race the 944 to make time over public roads—you just drive it quickly, that's all.

Technical Highlights

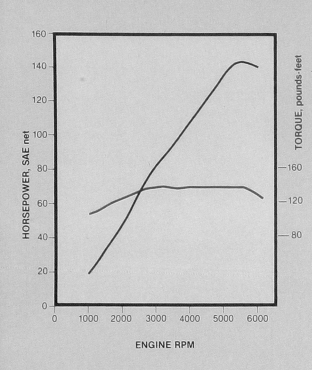

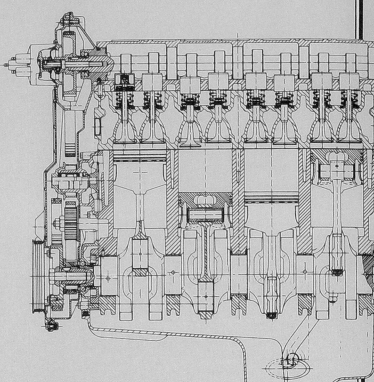

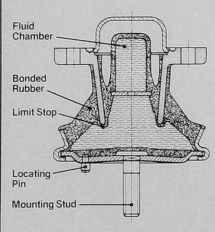

Engine Mount

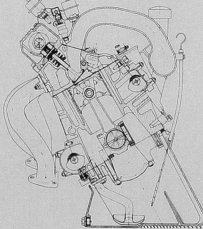

• The 924 is dead, after only seven years of production. Its demise, premature for a Porsche, was caused by its mediocre engine. The Audi-based powerplant was short on power and long on noise and vibration.

The 944 engine shows that these complaints eventually found sympathetic ears in Weissach. The new engine is basically one bank of a 928 V-8. Porsche's new four and its old eight share bore centers, cylinder-head-bolt spacing, Reynolds 390 die-cast-aluminum block construction (with linerless bores), aluminum cylinder heads with in-line valves and hydraulic

lifters, sintered connecting rods, and a one-piece main-bearing saddle with an integrally cast oil gallery. Most of the actual parts are slightly different, but the castings are frequently the same, and they're machined with the same tooling.

Displacing 2479cc, the 944 engine is 25 percent larger than its 1984cc predecessor. Horsepower is increased more than proportionally, from 110 to 143 (a 30 percent improvement), and torque is up from 111 to 137 pounds-feet (a 23 percent improvement). The 944's 3000-rpm torque-peaking speed is 500 rpm lower than the 924's, and its torque curve is flat

from 2500 to 5500 rpm.

Four-cylinder engines of this size normally shake like cement mixers. But Porsche engineers swallowed their pride in this case and purchased a license for twin balance shafts from Mitsubishi. The belt-driven shafts generate forces that cancel a four-cylinder's natural second-order (occurring at twice engine speed) vertical shaking forces. Positioned on either side of the block and vertically displaced, they also reduce the rocking movement inherent to four-cylinder engines. The balance shafts, originally patented by Frederick W. Lanchester of England in 1911, contribute eighteen pounds to the 330-pound engine weight and rob 4 hp at the peak, but they are still lighter and more efficient than the alternative of adding more cylinders.

Porsche has devised an innovative pair of engine mounts to take up where the balance shafts leave off in the struggle against roughness. Each mount is seated between an aluminum-alloy crossmember and a cast-aluminum engine bracket. Inside the rubber portion of each mount there are two antifreeze-filled cavities; a

And if you really want to press the limit, the 944 will not only let you, it will help you. The front end steers toward an apex easily—steering response is the one thing CN36 tires excel at—and as understeer builds up, the steering grows gradually heavier. At their low inflation pressures, the 944's front Pirellis squeal fairly easily, and if you enter a corner slowly and just turn the wheel you'll feel as if you're driving right over them. Enter a corner quickly, though, and it's another story. Trailing-throttle oversteer brings the rear end out just a touch to help point the front end toward the apex, and then the car's even weight distribution makes it easy to balance the 944 with gas pedal and steering wheel on the fast line. On the skidpad, the end result is 0.80 g, a respectable figure. But on the road, the result is magic, for there's one level of handling for everyday driving and another level for emergency maneuvers.

If you're looking for flaws in the 944, they do exist. The high bolsters of the leather sports seats fitted to this test car hold you in place, but they also emphasize the 944's lack of hiproom, make entry and exit from the driver's seat very difficult, and foul your elbows when you're working the steering wheel hard. The wheel still seems to sit in your lap,

no matter how small Porsche makes it. The Pirelli CN36 has been the rubber of choice for 924s since 1976, but it still rides too harshly even for this improved suspension. Furthermore, it isn't cheap. If you're looking for flaws, that's pretty much it. The rest is poetry.

Yet it's more than poetry that makes the 944 a great car. First, it's a great value. While "value" might be a difficult word to swallow in the same breath with a price just on the far side of $20,000, consider the facts. The price tag buys you a car with everything on it, from sunroof to air conditioning. All that's lacking is a radio to slot into the dash. The price tag also buys you a car that is comfortable on the Interstate and exquisitely exciting on a mountain road;

there's no need to shore up the 944's performance with selections from the options list. Moreover, your money buys you a car that's as fuel-efficient on the freeway as a Rabbit. Suddenly the 944 becomes the bargain of the decade.

The thing that really makes the 944 a terrific car, though, is the conviction of the engineers who made it that only performance matters. Not market position, not price, just performance. And as so often happens, dedication to a simple ideal has improved both market position and value. The result is the best combination of performance and economy that money can buy—a serious car that advances the state of the automotive art.

After all, that's what we expect from Porsche.

—*Michael Jordan*

separator plate between the two volumes has an orifice that allows the liquid to flow from one chamber to the other as the engine moves about. This back-and-forth flow produces damping forces much like a conventional shock absorber. As a result, the rubber mounts can be soft for good isolation and still maintain proper engine location.

After great strides had been made in comfort, Porsche engineers concentrated on maximizing the 944's fuel economy. The combustion chamber appears at a glance to be a conventional wedge, but it

benefits from Porsche's research into high compression with its TOP (thermally optimized performance) engine of a few years ago. The result is a fast-burn chamber that tolerates 9.5:1 compression even with America's low-octane unleaded fuels. Another fuel-economy plus is the Bosch Motronic engine-control system. This is Germany's version of the microprocessor engine controls common on American cars, although in the 944 it's coupled to port-type electronic fuel injection. It provides the same benefits of precise fuel metering and optimal spark tim

ing with minimal maintenance.

Now that the low end of the Porsche line has been plumped up with new power, the opportunity for great gains at the high end has also arrived. A V-8 version of the new 944 engine could theoretically produce 300 net horsepower and 280 pounds-feet of torque in emissions-legal trim. It could power a real 928S into the hearts and minds of car enthusiasts across the land. Such a 928, with the same sort of revitalization the 924 has just received, would be the fastest automobile available in America.

—*Csaba Csere*

22 Porsche 944

We live in an ocean of air. Seemingly, it offers no resistance as we walk through it. But, in fact, air does resist the forward movement of any object passing through it. Resistance increases with the square of the object's speed. And the power required to overcome it increases with the cube of the object's speed. Thus, even a small reduction in drag can improve both performance and efficiency.

To some, the best measure of a car's aerodynamic efficiency is its coefficient of drag, or C_d: a numerical value—the lower, the better—based on the ratio of the amount of wind resistance a car encounters to that encountered by a flat plate of the same size, facing perpendicular to the airflow.

At Porsche, based on years of racing experience, we believe a better measure is a car's *luftwiderstand:* an air resistance rating that is the product of $C_d \times F$ (where F is the car's frontal cross section in m^2).

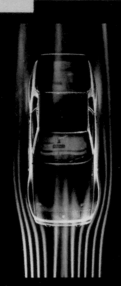

The 944 benefits from over 70 years of Porsche aerodynamic development. Its C_d is a low 0.35. And its F is a mere 1.82 m^2. As a result, its luftwiderstand is a highly favorable 0.637.

Because of the 944's design, while its 2.5-liter Porsche engine produces 143 hp at 5500 rpm, it requires only 13.9 hp to cruise at 55 mph. Thus, at maximum highway speed, the 944 has an unused reserve of 129.1 hp.

To combat aerodynamic lift forces which can adversely affect handling, the 944 is equipped with integral front and rear spoilers. In addition, the 944's transaxle design creates a high polar moment of inertia that resists cross-winds and increases directional control.

At Porsche, excellence is expected. For your dealer, call toll-free: (800) 447-4700.

PORSCHE + AUDI
NOTHING EVEN COMES CLOSE

RICHARD GEORGE

Far from Eden

*One of James Dean's favorite performances
was that of his Porsche Spyder. On September 30, 1955,
on a lonely stretch of California two-lane, he drove it to his death.*

BY BROCK YATES

• Welcome the silence. Break for a moment your bonds with time. You'll hear it first—the frantic growl of a four-cam Porsche. Unmuffled. Running hard. Look into the brown-weeded hills, where the old road winds around the edge of the ravine. A tiny silver Spyder squirts into sight, lashing through the apexes, its impudent snout nipping at the wooden guardrails. Stand back as it rushes past, scrabbling for traction on the scarred macadam. Follow its raucous exhaust. The two men in the cockpit—a slight young driver with clip-on sunglasses and a beefy passenger—lean slightly as the Porsche clears the final bend. It powers, clean and straight, speed building, toward the valley.

Far off, on the western slope, a stand of oaks marks the café at Cholame. But first there is the intersection where State 41 angles toward Fresno. A lone car is approaching, a black Ford two-door. It is slowing, readying for the turn. The Spyder hammers onward, a shiny aluminum pellet aglow in the late-afternoon sun. Surely the Ford will stop. Surely the driver will spot the speeding Porsche. Surely the world of heroes and dreamy idols will not be shattered on the road to Cholame . . .

James Dean opened big and died bigger. In death he had what the movie moguls call "legs"—that mysterious ability to endure in the face of critical assaults, the fevered promotion of rivals, and the notoriously fickle public.

Thirty years ago, at approximately 5:45 p.m. on the 30th of September, 1955, James Byron Dean, a 24-year-old actor with a single major screen role to his credit, crashed at the intersection of California routes 466 and 41, less than a mile east of Cholame. He died minutes later. It was the most famous highway accident in history. It thrust Dean into the pantheon of ritualized cult figures now occupied by the likes of Valentino, Monroe, JFK, Elvis, and John Lennon. None of them, not even Kennedy or Lennon or Presley, was mourned with more sound and fury and endless, hysterical weeping than James Dean.

The keepers of the flame will tell you he dreamed of being a Grand Prix driver and wheeling exotic sports cars from the time

JAMES DEAN

Above: Dean and Wütherich (center) check out the "Little Bastard" prior to the Salinas race. Right: Dean's move to California coincided with the height of the sports-car movement.

he was a surprisingly normal high-school kid in Fairmount, Indiana. Perhaps. Paul Newman, who knew Dean casually when both were trying to make it on the New York stage in the early 1950s, remembers no talk about automobiles. "We'd have a few beers and talk about acting," he recalls, "but I didn't care much about racing in those days and haven't any idea if he did or not. If he did, he didn't tell me about it."

What we do know is that Dean did not become a screen idol overnight. In the early Fifties he made a number of appearances in New York television dramas, got small parts in four long-forgotten pictures (*Has Anybody Seen My Gal?*, *Sailor Beware*, *Fixed Bayonets*, and *Trouble along the Way*), and earned strong reviews for his performance in Gide's *The Immoralist* on Broadway. His first major break in Hollywood came in March 1954 when he was cast as Cal Trask in Elia Kazan's production of John Steinbeck's *East of Eden*.

Although he had owned a couple of motorcycles, an old Harley and a 500cc Norton, Dean's plunge into the world of California sports cars did not come until a year later. In March 1955 he bought a white Porsche 356 Super Speedster from Johnny von Neumann's Competition Motors on North Vine Street in Hollywood. These were the halcyon days of the West Coast sports-car movement, with races being organized by the Sports Car Club of America and its rival, the California Sports Car Club, at seemingly every vacant airport between San Diego and San Francisco. Natu-

ral road circuits like Torrey Pines and Pebble Beach were also active, and plans were being formulated for permanent courses at places like Riverside and Laguna Seca. Everybody raced, or went to the races, or at the very least owned a tiny, two-seat sports car. To do otherwise was to risk social ruin. The serious drivers of the day—Phil Hill, Richie Ginther, Carroll Shelby, Bill Pollack, von Neumann, Ken Miles, Bob Drake, Bob Bondurant, and a blond prodigy from Riverside named Dan Gurney—competed in road races staged by both clubs. Dean joined the SCCA, but he attended few meetings and was known to the membership as just another young actor getting a short-burst publicity push from Warner Brothers.

Less than two weeks after buying the Porsche, he was a star. *East of Eden* opened well, and Dean received eloquent reviews. His introverted, renegade sensuality dominated the screen. One reviewer described this quality as the "innocent grace of a captive panther." Another called it "bastard robustness." Whatever it was, the skinny, slightly bowlegged former bongo player and track star from Fairmount High was the hottest property in show business. Warner Brothers immediately extended his contract and set him to work as the sullen, confused, misunderstood teen-ager in *Rebel without a Cause*. Before *Rebel* was completed, Warner announced that he would

star as Jett Rink, the rags-to-riches cowboy in Edna Ferber's *Giant*, then play Rocky Graziano, the fighter, in his screen biography, *Somebody up There Likes Me*. He was dating ravishing starlets like Pier Angeli and Ursula Andress, and he was driving fast. Very fast.

In late March Dean took the Speedster to the Palm Springs road races and won the novice event. Victory his first time out. He then ran in the main race for small-displacement cars and finished third behind the hot MG Specials of Ken Miles and Cy Yedor. When Miles was disqualified on a technicality, he advanced to second overall. Seriously myopic, Dean raced with a hunched, head-down ferocity that was complemented by a substantial talent. Dean was not some twit movie star out to impress his pals; he was ragged and over-eager, but he was far from slow. On May 1 he took the Porsche to a Cal Club event at Minter Field in Bakersfield and finished third in the 1300-to-2000cc Production class, again competing against more experienced drivers. His last race was on Memorial Day, 1955, at Santa Barbara, where he ran in the SCCA Under-1500cc Production class. After starting eighteenth, he charged all the way to fourth before the Porsche burned a piston.

Then it was over. Director George Ste-

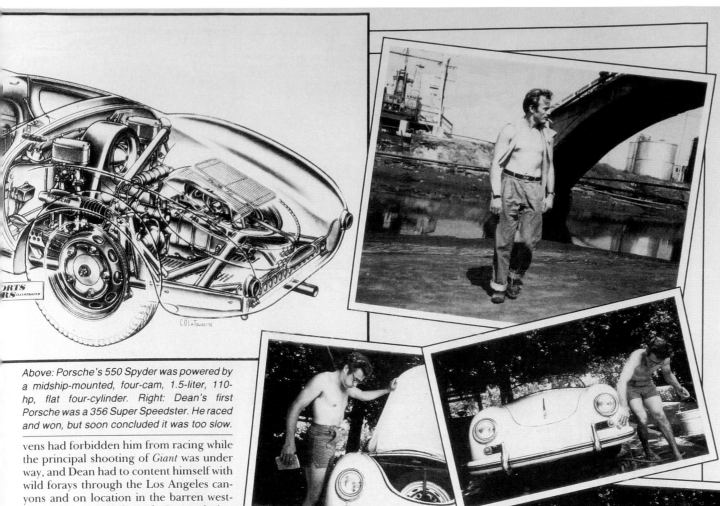

Above: Porsche's 550 Spyder was powered by a midship-mounted, four-cam, 1.5-liter, 110-hp, flat four-cylinder. Right: Dean's first Porsche was a 356 Super Speedster. He raced and won, but soon concluded it was too slow.

vens had forbidden him from racing while the principal shooting of *Giant* was under way, and Dean had to content himself with wild forays through the Los Angeles canyons and on location in the barren west-Texas range around Marfa. It was during this period, when the heady pressures of celebrity were beginning to bear on him, that word passed through the film colony: behind the wheel of his Porsche, James Dean was to be avoided like a subpoena to the House Un-American Activities Committee. He was a wild man, broadsliding the Speedster through the Hollywood streets like a stunt driver. It was then that he dismissed the 356 as too slow. When his *Giant* constraints were loosened, he would buy a serious race car.

Phil Hill remembers the day of Dean's death. Hill had been maintaining the graphite-gray three-liter Monza that he was driving for von Neumann at the Highland Avenue Ferrari agency, but his own rising celebrity status as America's most brilliant road racer had clogged the shop with oglers and hangers-on. Seeking privacy, he and mechanic Henry Pickett had taken the Monza to a small race shop owned by von Neumann on Ventura Boulevard. They were readying the car for a San Francisco region SCCA race, to be staged on October 1 at the airport at Salinas, a dusty town on the northern perimeter of the vast San Joaquin Valley. A produce center, it was best known as the birthplace of John Steinbeck.

Like most of the hard-core racers, Hill looked on Dean as an outsider. Also as an object of mystery, some faint jealousy, and not a little derision. He recalls Sam Wile, a partner of von Neumann's in the booming Porsche dealership and Volkswagen distributorship, announcing Dean's arrival to an amused office staff: "Here comes the Mickey Mouse Marlon Brando." Says Hill, "I felt he had enormous personal needs to be famous."

On September 17 Dean made a public-service television spot for the National Safety Council with actor Gig Young. He tagged it with a plea: "And remember, drive safely. The life you save may be mine." Four days later he went to Competition Motors and traded the Speedster for one of five Porsche 550 Spyders that von Neumann had imported directly from the factory. The tiny, aluminum-bodied racer, with a ladder frame and a midship-mounted four-cam, air-cooled four, was part of a batch of 75 that the factory had built for privateer racers that year. Dean's machine was to become the most famous—and mysterious—of the lot.

At the time, the 550 Spyder was the best small-displacement racer in the world. Not only was it quick and nimble, but its anvil-like reliability helped win many high placings in major endurance races. There was some question whether Dean was experienced enough for the machine, but on September 21 von Neumann accepted his check for $3000, plus the 356 Speedster in trade, for Spyder number 550-0055.

Dean took the car to Compton, where the well-known customizer George Barris added a bit of individuality. Stock Spyders were all silver, with only blue or red stripes atop the rear fenders (Dean's had red stripes). Barris painted "Little Bastard" in script across the tail and Dean's racing number, 130, on the doors, the hood, and the rear deck.

Jimmy, as his friends called him, took the Spyder to the streets, driving with customary fierceness. In the days before pollution controls and safety standards, a license could be tacked onto practically anything with four wheels, and so it was with the "Little Bastard." Several days later he had a minor shunt with a lady on Sunset Boulevard and returned the Porsche to Competition Motors for repairs.

At roughly the same time, Dean decided

that he would race at Salinas. (It must have been a last-hour decision, because the race program did not bear his name.) He had been there once before, on location for some of *East of Eden*. Dean had established a solid relationship with Rolf Wütherich, a 28-year-old German mechanic who had come to von Neumann's operation from the factory in Zuffenhausen; it was he who had prepared both the Speedster and the 550 for competition. Because the car was so fresh and the driver so inexperienced, Wütherich recommended that they drive the 300-odd miles to Salinas while someone else ferried Dean's 1953 Ford station wagon and a borrowed trailer for the return trip.

Dean was up early on the 30th, though he'd attended a party in Malibu the night before. He arrived at Competition Motors on North Vine a little after eight, having driven over the hill from his leased home at 14611 Sutton Street in Sherman Oaks. On the way he stopped at the Ventura Boulevard shop, where Hill and Pickett were laboring over the Monza. "It's the only time I ever talked with him, other than a few grunts at the racetrack," recalls Hill. "Generally, he'd show up with this great retinue of hangers-on, and I had no interest in that sort of thing. I needed to be a great racing driver, and that was my sole preoccupation. I'd seen dozens of these so-called godlike creatures from Hollywood, and I'd been inclined to treat him as sort of a mutation. But on that day we talked about racing without all the usual distractions."

Dean had lunch at the Farmer's Market with his father, Winton, and his uncle Charlie Nolan Dean. Shortly after lunch he met Wütherich at Competition Motors. The Spyder's engine was warming. Three friends were on hand: show-business pho-

Left: On location in Texas for shooting of <u>Giant</u> with Elizabeth Taylor, Dean, with amazing prescience, hogties his costar. Above: Dean's Spyder led a second life as an object lesson.

tographer Sanford Roth, stunt man Bill Hickman (who would make the famed drive for Steve McQueen in *Bullitt*), and Dean's insurance man, Lew Bracker. Roth and Hickman had been enlisted to dead-head the trailer to Salinas.

The route the racers took to the northern-California events was standard: Sepulveda Boulevard to 99 north over the notorious Grapevine and into the San Joaquin Valley; west on Route 166 toward Taft and Maricopa; then north on 33 to Blackwell's Corner. From there it was a flat shot west across the sagebrush-carpeted western end of the valley on old 466 into Paso Robles.

Dean was issued a speeding ticket on Grapevine. He stopped for a soft drink and an apple at a café in Blackwell's Corner ("elevation 278 ft., rainfall 8 drops, population 9002 . . . 9000 squirrels, 2 humans"), where he chatted with Lance Reventlow, who was on the way to Salinas in a new Mercedes-Benz 300SL gull-wing. They agreed to meet for dinner in Paso Robles.

No one knows how quickly Dean traversed the run from Blackwell's Corner toward Cholame. Some speculate that he was running the deserted road at his customary frantic pace. Others say no, that the fresh race engine that had to be run in, plus the presence of Wütherich, the factory-trained veteran of Le Mans, Reims, and the Mille Miglia, would have imposed restraint. We know this much: He zoomed over the barren Diablo Range where the San Andreas Fault, looking like the clenched jaws of a half-buried dragon, borders the road, and through what the locals call Polonio Pass. He charged at the valley floor to the east of Cholame far in front of Roth and Hickman in the wagon. As he hit the straight, he was probably loafing the Porsche at 80 to 85 mph.

Heading east was a 23-year-old student from California Polytechnic in San Luis Obispo named Donald Turnupseed. He was driving his 1950 Ford home to Fresno for the weekend. He would have to make a left turn off of 466 where Route 41 angled northeast. A left turn directly in front of the approaching Spyder.

According to Wütherich, James Dean's last words were, "He's gotta see us. He's gotta stop."

Turnupseed did not stop. He turned left. At the last second he spotted the tiny car. He spiked the brakes. Dean apparently tried to drive around the Ford and never braked. The Spyder took the full impact of the Ford's blunt grille in the left door. The impact threw Wütherich into the air and clear of the wreck. Dean was crammed against the steering wheel and mauled by the intruding Ford nose. Turnupseed was

dazed and bloodied from the impact but essentially unhurt.

A sharp screech of brakes, the hollow report of imploding aluminum, and it was over. James Byron Dean had driven himself into the Valhalla of fallen idols.

Phil Hill was about two hours behind. He came upon the accident site long after the Porsche and the Ford had been hauled to a little Quonset-hut garage in Cholame. Dean's body had been taken to the Kuehl funeral home in Paso Robles while surgeons at the local hospital were deciding whether or not to amputate Wütherich's left leg. Turnupseed told the police he simply had not seen the Porsche, and he was not charged. Hill recalls seeing parked cars and masses of smoking flares and flashing lights arcing in the desert night. After being informed of the crash, he and Pickett drove on to Salinas. Von Neumann and his wife Eleanor had passed through earlier. They had arrived at the moment the Spyder was being hoisted onto the back of a tow truck, and they had asked a policeman if Dean had been hurt. The officer replied, "Yeah, he's been hurt real bad. He's dead." They proceeded to Salinas, unaware that their employee Wütherich had also been in the car.

The coroner's report reveals that Dean suffered a broken neck, coupled with multiple fractures of the jaw and both arms. He clung to life for a few minutes after the crash, then died in the ambulance en route to the hospital in Paso Robles. (One ghoulish footnote: there was not enough blood left to complete a blood-alcohol test, though there was no reason to believe

JAMES DEAN

This monument to Dean stands about a mile away from the crash site, in Cholame. "Death," said Dean, "is the one inevitable, undeniable truth."

JAMES DEAN
1931Feb8—1955Sep30pm5:59 ∞

that he had been drinking.)

Within an hour the news was being spread, first by KPRL in Paso Robles, then by word of mouth, and finally by the major media around the world. Considering that his celebrity status could be measured in months, not years, the death of James Dean gained an energy and a mystique unlike any other. Four weeks later, *Rebel without a Cause* opened in New York. Two weeks after that, *Giant* premièred there. Both pictures were hits, certainly in part because of the pathos surrounding the young star. That was only the beginning. One year following his death, James Dean was listed as the number-one box-office attraction by *Photoplay* magazine and was still the intended recipient of 1000 fan letters a week. Rumors swirled about his committing suicide after losing Pier Angeli to Vic Damone; about a fortuneteller's prediction of doom; about his surviving the accident and living as a disfigured recluse. All of this was nonsense.

As for Wütherich, he was transported back to Los Angeles by von Neumann, where his leg was saved. However, he never returned to normal. Obsessed with the crash, he continued to work for various

West Coast Porsche operations until he became moody and unruly. Finally, the factory returned him to Germany, where he worked with the testing department at Zuffenhausen. On July 28, 1981, he skidded on a wet road in Kupferzell, West Germany, a few miles from his birthplace in Heilbronn, and was killed.

Donald Turnupseed reportedly settled in the Fresno area. No doubt concerned with protecting himself and his family from lunatic avengers, he has refused to discuss the accident publicly.

As for Porsche Spyder 550-0055, this much is known: The wreck was taken to San Luis Obispo, where racing enthusiast Dr. William Eschrich of Burbank removed the undamaged engine and transaxle. The engine was briefly front-mounted in his Lotus 9, without great success, and remains in the doctor's possession. The transaxle is now owned by a collector in Piedmont, California, but the whereabouts of the rest of the car are unknown.

George Barris obtained the wreck shortly after the crash. (Some implied that it was a "jinx" car, citing the case of Dr. Troy McHenry, who used the car's trailing arms on a special in which he crashed fatally at Pomona; but the cause was the failure of a non-Porsche part.) Historians believe that, after some efforts to unkink the frame and bodywork, Barris turned the car over to the Greater Los Angeles Safety Council. It was placed on a nationwide tour, intended to scare young Dean worshipers into driving sensibly.

This gruesome exhibit meandered around the nation for four years, until 1960 when it was put on a train in Florida to be returned to California. The car was stolen somewhere in the Midwest, and it has not been seen since. Some speculate

that it was sawed into souvenir bits. Others believe it is in the hands of a private collector. Perhaps it is rotting in some backwater barn. Lee Raskin, a prominent Porsche historian who has extensively researched the subject, wonders whether Dean's family, tiring of the notoriety, had the car stolen and destroyed.

Old Route 466 to Cholame is closed. It lies, weed-pocked and barricaded, to the south of new Highway 46. The intersection has been altered, and there is no sure way of locating the exact point of the crash. On a phone pole is nailed a wind-tattered picture of the "Little Bastard." A mile away, in Cholame (population 65), the scene is essentially unchanged from 1955. Aggie's Restaurant, next to the garage where the Porsche was taken, serves hamburgers and features Hank Williams on the jukebox. A faded poster recounts the life of James Dean. In front of the post office next door, where postmistress Lilly Grant acts as the unofficial curator of the local Dean memorabilia, stands a stainless-steel monument surrounding a tree of heaven. The marker, erected in 1977 by a Tokyo businessman, Seita Ohnishi, who is the proprietor of a Dean souvenir business both here and in Japan, reflects the crash site in its polished surface. Mrs. Grant watches from the door of her tiny post office as dozens of motorists stop each day to visit the memorial. Engraved on its surface is this simple notation: "James Dean, 1931Feb8–1955Sep30pm5:59."

Surrounding the monument on a low stone wall is a series of plaques containing sayings by Dean and by André Gide and others whom Dean is said to have favored. One has been ripped up and carried away. One, which some say was Dean's favorite, is a quotation from *The Little Prince:* "What is essential is invisible to the eye." There is another that seems more appropriate, especially considering that its author was James Byron Dean himself:

"Death is the one inevitable, undeniable truth. In it lies the only ultimate nobility for man. Beyond it, through immortality, the only hope." ●

Porsche 959

Twenty-four hours in sports-car heaven.

• We hesitate to call any car perfect. The absence of flaws in any product of human endeavor is extraordinarily rare. But we have just returned from West Germany, where we finally got a chance to drive a Porsche 959 on the street, and the word "perfect" is difficult to avoid. What single word more accurately describes a car that combines race-car performance with luxury-sedan comfort, that is equally adept at commuting through rush-hour traffic, profiling in jet-set locales, negotiating blizzard-swept mountain passes, and outrunning light airplanes? The Porsche 959 can accomplish almost any automotive mission so well that to call it

perfect is the mildest of overstatements.

Power and speed are the core of the 959's excellence. With rocket-sled acceleration and the highest top end we've ever measured, the 959 stands alone at the pinnacle of production-car performance. If that sounds like hyperbole, how does a 0-to-60-mph time of 3.6 seconds strike you? Or 100 mph from rest in a mere 8.8 seconds, 120 mph in 12.4 seconds, and 140 mph in a tick less than 20 seconds? The 959 devours the standing quarter-mile in twelve seconds flat, with a terminal speed of 116 mph.

We recorded these figures at the Hockenheim-Ring, the site of this year's

German Grand Prix, employing a starting procedure recommended by Manfred Bantle, the project director of the 959 program. The drill was to switch the 959's programmable four-wheel-drive system into its locked setting, engage low gear, wind the engine to 7000 rpm, and drop the clutch. The result was a cloud of rubber dust from four spinning Bridgestone RE71 gumballs, and a car that disappeared as if shot from a cannon.

As remarkable as these acceleration runs were, the 959 was just as impressive when accelerated in a more normal fashion. In tests with no wheelspin and minimal clutch slip, it sprinted from rest to 60

PHOTOGRAPHY BY MARTYN GODDARD

mph in only 4.9 seconds.

Unlike most ultraperformance cars, the 959 is astonishingly easy to drive. This is especially true if one starts in the lowest of the transmission's six ratios—though Porsche, inexplicably, discourages this practice in on-road driving by labeling the bottom gear with a "G," for *Gelände* (terrain). When starting off in "G," minimal clutch slip is needed to help the engine onto its power band. The clutch action is on the heavy side but very progressive, and stirring the shifter is a delight. The lever has been moved about three inches rearward from the usual 911 location, and the linkage has none of the rubbery feel we've come to expect in rear-engined cars. Instead, the 959 shifts with a wonderfully slick and fluid action. And with six ratios to choose from, the driver can run the engine either mild or wild.

These two personalities are clearly defined by the transition from single- to twin-turbo operation. The 959's engine—all 24 valves, four overhead camshafts, twin turbochargers and intercoolers, two water-cooled heads, and six titanium connecting rods of it—is essentially a domesticated version of the 962's racing powerhouse. Such engines thrive at high rpm but generally are weak at low engine speeds. The solution in the 959 is a staged turbocharger system. At low rpm, all of the exhaust flow is directed through just one turbocharger, bringing it quickly up to speed. Boost starts to build at 1500 rpm; by about 3000 rpm, the peak pressure of 14.5 psi is available. The second turbocharger cuts in at about 4300 rpm, uncorking the engine's high-speed breathing abilities. The 959, in turn, surges forward as if a second set of cylinders were activated.

Developing 444 hp at 6500 rpm, the 959's 2.8 liter flat six-cylinder produces more than 156 hp per liter. To put that into perspective, the Callaway Corvette's twin-turbo V-8 has twice the displacement of the 959 engine but produces about 100 hp less, for a specific output of only 60 hp per liter.

In spite of its heroic output, the 959's all-aluminum powerplant is always smooth and refined. It idles evenly at 800 rpm, it can be driven away at 1000 rpm in top gear without a shudder or a lurch, and it's quieter than a production 911 powerplant. When it climbs into the boost mode, its power surge feels like a strong push rather than a hard punch. This softness around the edges of the awesome power curve lets the driver use the 959's tremendous thrust with confidence.

Project director Bantle believes strongly that speed without security and stability is senseless, and we were eager to see whether his car would deliver both elements of the equation. The 959 was in our hands for only 24 hours, so we had no time to find a track where we could measure its top speed. We had to do it the German way—on the autobahn. We chose to

A small planetary gearbox and a preset torque wrench are used to apply the specified 625 pound-feet of torque to the wheels' central locking nuts.

run at night, when traffic was minimal, but the conditions were less than ideal: our test stretch was only two lanes wide, and it wasn't perfectly straight. Nevertheless, we clocked a two-way average of 190 mph, without ever feeling as though we were driving on the hairy edge. According to the factory, the 959 will do 195 if given enough room.

Driving at such speeds is completely comfortable in the 959. Porsche claims that it develops no aerodynamic lift at high speed, and we have no reason to doubt that. In our testing the 959 never felt light, and it always tracked straight and true. Neither side winds nor the wakes of slow-moving trucks seemed able to deflect it from its path.

Indeed, every aspect of the 959 promotes confidence in its high-speed abilities. The power steering has the pronounced self-centering of a 928. Tight door and glass seals limit wind noise. The brakes are powerful and fade-free no mat-

ter how hard or at what speed they're applied. At almost any cruising speed, the engine seems to be loafing. And the control-arm suspension keeps a tight rein on body motions but still absorbs bumps with supple strokes. In fact, the 959 rides more comfortably than the 911.

In addition to its superb high-speed stability, the 959 is an extremely capable back-road runner. Although it doesn't turn in with the sharpness of, say, a Z51 Corvette, it responds very progressively to the helm and exerts a tenacious grip on the pavement. We tested it on both a 197-foot and a 633-foot skidpad at Porsche's Weissach facility and measured lateral accelerations of 0.87 and 0.89 g, respectively. Controllability at the limit was excellent. Too much power and the car understeered; backing off of the throttle diminished the understeer and kept the tail obediently in line.

We further explored the 959's handling on the short course at Hockenheim. The

only way we could make its tail swing wide was to brake hard and late into corners. We could then hold the tail out with power, but the chassis was unstable in that attitude. It was much more rewarding to enter a corner conservatively, then take advantage of the four-wheel drive and the tires' prodigious grip by applying power early and exiting very fast. The same approach worked nicely on the road as well.

Much of the credit for the 959's unparalleled combination of performance and refinement must go to the high technology incorporated in its design. In this respect the 959 stands in stark contrast to certain Italian exoticars, in which electronic fuel injection is still something of a novelty. The Porsche's blend of low-speed refinement and high-end power would be impossible without its Bosch Motronic engine-control system to optimize fuel metering, ignition timing, and turbocharger boost for all operating conditions. Likewise, its unusually broad

118

power band could not have been achieved without the staged turbocharger setup.

Technology also serves to harness this considerable power. The Porsche "Control Coupling" four-wheel-drive system distributes power to the wheels according to the dynamic loading on the tires, providing extraordinary stability and handling consistency at all speeds. The damping of the three-position shock absorbers increases progressively with speed to provide proper ride control without excessive harshness. Automatic ride-height control allows the springs to be calibrated for handling without regard to the vagaries of payloads and vertical aerodynamic forces. And the 959's tire-pressure-monitoring system ought to discourage its drivers from trying to set speed records when their tires are underinflated.

Not only do these advanced technical features work well, but every detail of the 959 has been fine-tuned to the nth degree. In view of the car's very limited production, it's amazing how well developed it is. The 959's body and chassis are as solid as any on the road. The wind noise, mechanical vibration, and road rumble that intrude into its cabin are remarkably well attenuated. Its air conditioning, power windows and seats, sound system, and other luxury features work as well as any Cadillac's. Such special details as aerodynamically efficient, wide-angle exterior mirrors and telescoping headlight washers have been fully developed. There is even a fist-sized planetary-gearbox adapter to make it easier to apply the correct amount of torque to the magnesium wheels' central locking nuts.

We did detect a few flaws during our 24 hours with the 959. Its ancestry is all too apparent in its dashboard layout, which adds several controls to the 911's already haphazard arrangement of switches. Its power brakes are a trifle sensitive to the first portion of pedal travel. Its power steering feels somewhat artificial, with limited feedback from the front tires in corners. And its stock 911 seats provide too little lumbar support.

The most disturbing flaw of all is that you can't buy a 959. Not even if you have enough money—nearly a quarter of a million dollars—stuffed under your mattress. Porsche has sold out the entire production run of 200 cars (none of which was built to American specifications), and it does not intend to build any more.

In price, in availability, in performance, the 959 defies comparison with lesser machinery. The ultimate automobile, it is to any ordinary car as the F-15 is to a hang glider. We cannot, in the final analysis, call it perfect. But if you want to call the Porsche 959 the best car in the world, you will get no argument from us.

—Csaba Csere

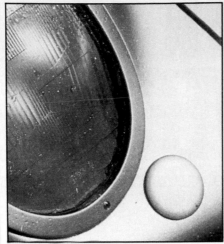

The 959's telescoping headlight washers lie flush until activated, then rise to the occasion.

Vehicle type: rear-engine, 4-wheel-drive, 2 + 2-passenger, 2-door coupe

Price as tested: $227,000 (West Germany)

Options on test car: none

Standard accessories: power steering, windows, seats, and locks, A/C, rear defroster

Sound system: Blaupunkt Bremen AM/FM-stereo radio/cassette, 4 speakers

ENGINE

Type	turbocharged and intercooled flat 6, aluminum block, cylinders, and heads
Bore x stroke	3.74 x 2.64 in, 95.0 x 67.0mm
Displacement	174 cu in, 2849cc
Compression ratio	8.3:1
Engine-control system	Bosch Motronic with port fuel injection
Turbochargers	2 KKK
Waste gates	2 Porsche
Maximum boost pressure	14.5 psi
Valve gear	chain-driven double overhead cams, 4 valves per cylinder, hydraulic lifters
Power (SAE net)	444 bhp @ 6500 rpm
Torque (SAE net)	369 lb-ft @ 5500 rpm

DRIVETRAIN

Transmission 6-speed
Final-drive ratio .... 4.13:1, limited slip

Gear	Ratio	Mph/1000 rpm	Max. test speed
I	3.50	5.0	37 mph (7300 rpm)
II	2.06	8.5	62 mph (7300 rpm)
III	1.41	12.5	91 mph (7300 rpm)
IV	1.04	17.0	124 mph (7300 rpm)
V	0.81	22.0	161 mph (7300 rpm)
VI	0.64	28.0	190 mph (6800 rpm)

DIMENSIONS AND CAPACITIES

Wheelbase	89.4 in
Track, F/R	59.2/61.0 in
Length	167.7 in
Width	72.4 in
Height	47.2 in

Frontal area	20.7 sq ft
Ground clearance	4.7 in
Curb weight	3500 lb
Weight distribution, F/R	40/60%
Fuel capacity	23.8 gal
Oil capacity	19.0 qt
Water capacity	26.4 qt

CHASSIS/BODY

Type	unit construction
Body material	welded steel stampings, aluminum stampings, Kevlar- and fiberglass-reinforced plastic

INTERIOR

SAE volume, front seat	43 cu ft
rear seat	13 cu ft
trunk space	2 cu ft
Front seats	bucket
Seat adjustments	fore and aft, seatback angle, front height, rear height
General comfort	poor fair **good** excellent
Fore-and-aft support	poor fair **good** excellent
Lateral support	poor fair **good** excellent

SUSPENSION

F:	ind, unequal-length control arms, coil springs, anti-roll bar
R:	ind, unequal-length control arms, coil springs, anti-roll bar

STEERING

Type	rack-and-pinion, power-assisted
Turns lock-to-lock	2.9
Turning circle curb-to-curb	36.4 ft

BRAKES

F:	12.7 x 1.3-in vented disc
R:	12.0 x 1.1-in vented disc
Power assist	hydraulic with anti-lock control

WHEELS AND TIRES

Wheel size	F: 8.0 x 17 in; R: 9.0 x 17 in
Wheel type	cast magnesium, center-lock hubs
Tires	Bridgestone RE71, F: 235/45VR-17; R: 255/40VR-17
Test inflation pressures, F/R	39/46 psi

CAR AND DRIVER TEST RESULTS

ACCELERATION	Seconds
Zero to 30 mph	1.5
40 mph	2.2
50 mph	2.9
60 mph	3.6
70 mph	4.8
80 mph	5.8
90 mph	7.1
100 mph	8.8
110 mph	10.4
120 mph	12.4
130 mph	15.9
140 mph	19.9
Top-gear passing time, 30–50 mph	11.9
50–70 mph	8.8
Standing ¼-mile	12.0 sec @ 116 mph
Top speed	190 mph

BRAKING
70–0 mph @ impending lockup .... 166 ft
Fade .... **none** moderate heavy

HANDLING
Roadholding, 197-ft-dia skidpad .... 0.87 g
Understeer .... minimal **moderate** excessive

FUEL ECONOMY
C/D observed fuel economy .... **13 mpg**

INTERIOR SOUND LEVEL
Idle .... 56 dBA
Full throttle acceleration .... 83 dBA
70-mph cruising .... 71 dBA
70-mph coasting .... 70 dBA

'97 IMPORTS

Porsche
Boxster

The winner, by a knockout.

BY PETER ROBINSON

If there has been a contest going on among BMW, Mercedes-Benz, and Porsche to see which German automaker could build the best-performing small roadster, Porsche should be passing out cigars right now. The new mid-engined Boxster is all Porsche, a simply marvelous sports car and the most dynamic and exciting of all the new generation of two-seat roadsters.

Where the BMW Z3 is soft and affordable and the Mercedes SLK so civilized it's hedonistic, the Boxster is pure, taut, and sparkling with desirability.

It is also the first truly new Porsche road car in 19 years. Nothing about its mid-engined layout, its MacPherson-strut suspension, or its water-cooled boxer engine is revolutionary, but all these pieces are new to the Boxster and share nothing with the 33-year-old 911 model or the 968 or 928 cars. This is one of those rare new-from-the-ground-up designs.

Many observers had expected the Boxster to be a severely watered-down version of the beautiful, show-stealing concept car Porsche unveiled in 1993. The show car lacked luggage space, didn't own a roof of any kind, and wouldn't have passed 1993 federal crashworthiness tests, let alone side-impact and head-protection standards.

But see this Boxster in the flesh, and it tells you the show car hasn't been compromised. Yes, it's 7.9 inches longer (all in the overhangs) than that show car, also 1.5 inches wider and a tad higher, but the benefits of a fabric top that retracts in 12 seconds at the push of a button—plus two sensibly large luggage compartments—can't be denied. Nor can a roomy cockpit with the driver's seat, steering wheel, and pedals all in perfect alignment—something no previous Porsche has ever achieved.

But where the Boxster really needed to deliver was on the road. It does, brilliantly.

At first, the messages are confusing. Driving away from the Weissach development center in Germany, we found the Boxster subdued, relaxed, refined. It doesn't sound like a Porsche. At least, not yet. Only a long and clumsy clutch travel spoils this perception of civility, and the throttle lacks the instant, gutsy responsiveness of the 968. This new engine, always tractable and silky smooth, is at its best between 4000 rpm and the 6600-rpm redline.

Porsche developed this new flat-six for the Boxster and, in 3.4-liter form, for next year's 996 replacement for the 911. All it shares with the 33-year-old 3.6-liter air-cooled six is the same 118-mil-

75

Front cubbyhole, at left below, and rear trunk combined carry 9.1 cubic feet of luggage. Above at left, the best—and only—view of the engine is from beneath a hydraulic lift; "service bay" is in the trunk.

limeter (4.65 inch) bore spacing. Water cooling was required to cope with the intense heat generated in the four-valves-per-cylinder heads. Water cooling also simplifies the task of meeting stringent new emissions standards. The new engine features a forged crankshaft running on seven main bearings. As equipped for the Boxster, the aluminum 24-valve 2.5-liter pumps out 201 horsepower at 6000 rpm and 180 pound-feet of torque at a peaky 4500 rpm, though Porsche hastens to note that variable intake-valve timing helps to provide at least 147 pound-feet from 1750 rpm all the way to 6500 rpm.

Oddly enough, the engine cover is not removable. Your bonding with the engine is done through a small service bay in the rear trunk that allows fluid levels to be checked and replenished. Still, the company claims this will be the cheapest Porsche to service.

Performance-wise, the Boxster easily outshines BMW's new Z3 and the Benz SLK, though its appeal goes way beyond the claimed 6.7-second 0-to-60 time (7.4 for the Boxster equipped with the five-speed Tiptronic) and 149-mph top speed with the manual. As the

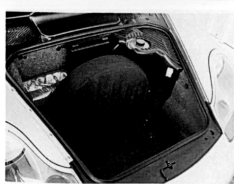

Removable wind blocker, at right, gives big hair a fighting chance. Spoiler on rear deck pops up automatically when happy driver reaches 76 mph.

retro-style tach needle—it's directly in front of the driver, just like the 911's—spins above the numeral "4," the engine comes alive. At 5200 rpm, it delivers a passionate howl and hurls the car forward toward an even deeper wail at 6000 rpm. It's the sound of a fanatically eager engine, which should go a long way toward justifying the Boxster's $45,000 price.

You quickly discover that the engine concerto is only one element in a fusion of talents that combine perfectly to turn every corner into an event, every driver into a hero. Low weight helps. At 2750 pounds, the base Boxster is 250 pounds lighter than the less powerful SLK. That's partly because the Boxster doesn't have the SLK's folding steel roof, but it's also the result of Porsche's using a variety of exotic materials: magnesium roll bars; an aluminum engine, suspension, and brakes; and an optional aluminum hard top that weighs just 55 pounds.

The weight is carefully balanced, with 48 percent on the front wheels. Packaging constraints led to the use of MacPherson struts front and rear, rather than control arms. The suspension is designed to provide negative toe-in at the outer front wheel and positive toe-in at the outer rear wheel to improve stability and to err on the side of understeer.

The rack-and-pinion, power-assisted steering has virtually the same ratio as the 911's, but the Boxster's 2.3-inch-wider track allows an extra half-turn of steering lock that tightens its turning circle by 2.8 feet despite its 5.5-inch-longer wheelbase.

The suspension is taut, but it still delivers a quiet and compliant ride. It feels nimble, responsive, and agile—as expected of a mid-engined car—but it's also stable and predictable up to, and at, the very high limits of adhesion. Not that finding those limits was easy on our test car, which was shod with the optional

205/50ZR-17 front and 255/40ZR-17 rear Pirelli P Zero Asimmetricos (16-inch wheels are standard).

Imagine this in a Porsche: You can dive deep into a tight second-gear corner, back off, even brake if you like, and the Boxster doesn't deviate off the line. Its handling character is almost completely neutral, and yet small course corrections can be made with the throttle.

Four massive monoblock cast calipers, each with four pistons, clamp down hard on vented discs with the assistance of anti-lock brakes to give a positive pedal feel and staggering stopping power. Porsche's switchable traction control is optional.

The Boxster is not just a pretty shape, but a slippery one, too—Porsche claims its 0.31 Cd sets a record for a roadster. A smooth underbody helps to reduce front-end lift by 36 percent. To minimize rear lift, a small lip positioned between the rear

trunklid and bumper automatically rises 3.1 inches when speeds climb above 75 mph.

The Boxster—available here in January—represents a return to the company's original philosophies, wrapped in an entirely contemporary design. No other roadster offers the same dazzling blend of performance, handling, ride, and refinement. Yes, it is dynamically superior to the classic 911, though it is not quite as quick.

How things have changed for Porsche. Just five years ago, the company was well on its way toward developing a four-door sedan, the 989, a $90,000 luxury car with sporting connotations. At the time, the Boxster did not exist. But at the end of 1991, there was a palace revolt in the board room and a resulting 180-degree shift in direction. The 989 was dropped, and Porsche went back to basics. The engineers wondered about a front-engined replacement for the 944/968 but eventually decided real Porsches use a boxer engine, located somewhere behind the driver. The Boxster is dazzling evidence that they were right. ●

PORSCHE BOXSTER

Vehicle type: mid-engine, rear-wheel-drive, 2-passenger, 2-door roadster

Estimated base price: $45,000

Engine type: DOHC 24-valve flat-6, aluminum block and heads, DME M5.2 engine-control system with port fuel injection

Displacement	151 cu in, 2480cc
Power (SAE net)	201 bhp @ 6000 rpm
Torque (SAE net)	180 lb-ft @ 4500 rpm
Transmission	5-speed manual or 5-speed automatic with lockup torque converter
Wheelbase	95.0 in
Length	169.9 in
Width	70.0 in
Height	50.8 in
Curb weight	2750–2800 lb

Manufacturer's performance ratings:	manual	auto
Zero to 60 mph, seconds	6.7	7.4
Top speed (drag limited), mph	149	146
Projected fuel economy:	**manual**	**auto**
European city cycle, mpg	19	—
Steady 56 mph, mpg	37	35
Steady 75 mph, mpg	29	28

56

COMPARISON TEST

Spring Fancies

Spring has sprung, the sap is rising, and—heh, heh—it's time to hug a few curves.

BY PATRICK BEDARD

"**I**n the spring a young man's fancy lightly turns to thoughts of love," wrote Alfred, Lord Tennyson. Easy for him to say—sports cars weren't much of a distraction in 1842. But this spring, we predict, love is in for tough competition from the niftiest class of two-seaters to come along in a beagle's age.

Sports cars had a good year in 1990, when, all by itself, the new Mazda Miata had the chattering classes wound up for about a year and a half. Remembering way back, 1970 stands out, too, for the simultaneous arrival of the fastback Datsun 240Z and the lump-shaped Porsche 914. But 1997's class of four outshines them all—three radically new models plus a celebrated yearling fresh from steroid therapy.

The yearling is, of course, the BMW Z3 2.8, looking all muscled up now that its rear fenders have been stretched over a wider rear track. What you don't see is the *real* muscle. The 189-horsepower six-cylinder from the 328 sedan fills the long engine bay (continued is the four-cylinder version for those under doctor's order to limit their cardiac excitement).

Topping the radically new list is the Mercedes-Benz SLK. This deftly engineered two-seater packs a supercharged four-cylinder up front and a single red button on the console that transforms the car from snug coupe to open roadster in one touch of one finger. So impressed are we by this SLK that we unhesitatingly voted it to a spot on our 1997 Ten Best list.

Radically new, too, not to mention *long awaited*, describes the Porsche Boxster. Twenty-some years later, Porsche finally makes amends for the unfortunate 914 with a middle-motor sportster that really works.

The terms "radically new" and "long awaited" apply equally well to the fourth member of 1997's sports-car class, the all-new Chevrolet Corvette. But does that magnum-caliber V-8 Detroiter belong in the same group with these compact Europeans? If price is all that counts—each one lists for about 40 large—then you'd have to say yes. But whether you're buying fine wines, politicians, or sports cars, price is never all that counts. The talent and swagger and thrust of the Corvette flow from a philosophy that is very much different from the others. Besides, the '97 Corvette is a targa, not a true convertible.

When the '98-model convertible arrives, we may toss it into

PHOTOGRAPHY BY DAVID DEWHURST

Mercedes-Benz SLK

Highs: Cheeky good looks, tremendous road grip, draft-free with the roof up, one finger puts the roof down.

Lows: The five-speed is a (groan) automatic, the grip reaches its limit with too little warning.

The Verdict: Only an unreconstructed sports-car nut would find this machine lacking.

the mix. Right now, we have a trio of German two-seaters seductive enough to lure Tennyson back for a rewrite of his famous line. Let's see how the test drivers' fancy turns as we put each one through a springtime romp.

Third Place
Mercedes-Benz SLK

We still admire the SLK every bit as much as we did when naming it to our

1997 Ten Best list at the beginning of the year. And for exactly the same reasons. "Does the SLK stand as the optimum realization of the concept?" we asked in our January road test. "Darn near," we answered. "But let's be clear. The concept isn't Sports Car. The SLK is more like the slam-dunk champ in a league of one."

The SLK concept is this: a cockpit tightly sealed against weather and noise when the top is up; a fully automated one-

touch, 25-second retraction of that top; and an exceptionally shake-and-rattle-free ride when the top is down. What you get is the best of both the coupe and convertible worlds, and a painless transition between the two, a state of excellence no true sports car has yet to match. Oh, yes, and don't forget the hey-look-at-me styling that confers instant celebrity on its driver.

Still, any two-seater must inevitably be held up to the sports-car yardstick. When

C/D Test Results

	0–30 mph	0–60 mph	0–100 mph	0–120 mph	1/4-mile	street start, 5–60 mph	top gear, 30–50 mph	top gear, 50–70 mph	top speed, mph	braking, 70–0 mph, feet	roadholding, 300-foot skidpad, g
							acceleration, seconds				
BMW Z3 2.8	2.0	6.3	18.3	37.2	14.9 @ 92 mph	7.0	8.5	8.2	129 (governed)	171	0.87
MERCEDES-BENZ SLK	2.5	7.2	20.0	33.1	15.5 @ 91 mph	7.6	3.7	5.2	144	170	0.90
PORSCHE BOXSTER	2.1	6.2	17.5	31.1	14.8 @ 93 mph	7.1	10.6	11.0	145	179	0.81
TEST AVERAGE	*2.2*	*6.6*	*18.6*	*33.8*	*15.1 @ 92 mph*	*7.2*	***	***	*139*	*173*	*0.86*

*The automatic SLK downshifts in this test, so the numbers are not comparable with the fifth-gear acceleration times of the Z3 and Boxster.

Vital Statistics

	price, base/ as tested	engine	SAE net power/torque	transmission/ gear ratios:1/ maximum test speed, mph/ axle ratio:1	curb weight, pounds	weight distribution, % front/rear
BMW Z3 2.8	$36,668/ $37,423	DOHC 24-valve 6-in-line, 170 cu in (2793cc), aluminum block and head, Siemens MS 41.0 engine-control system with port fuel injection	189 bhp @ 5300 rpm/ 203 lb-ft @ 3950 rpm	5-speed manual/ 4.20, 2.49, 1.66, 1.24, 1.00/ 34, 58, 86, 116, 129/ 3.15	2920	52.1/47.9
MERCEDES-BENZ SLK	$41,123/ $42,095	supercharged and intercooled DOHC 16-valve 4-in-line, 140 cu in (2295cc), iron block and aluminum head, Bosch ME 2.1 engine-control system with port fuel injection	185 bhp @ 5300 rpm/ 200 lb-ft @ 3650 rpm	5-speed auto, lockup converter/ 3.93, 2.41, 1.49, 1.00, 0.83/ 32, 53, 86, 127, 144/ 3.27	3020	53.6/46.4
PORSCHE BOXSTER	$41,284/ $41,673	DOHC 24-valve flat-6, 151 cu in (2480cc), aluminum block and heads, Bosch DME engine-control system with port fuel injection	201 bhp @ 6000 rpm/ 181 lb-ft @ 4500 rpm	5-speed manual/ 3.50, 2.12, 1.43, 1.03, 0.79/ 34, 56, 83, 116, 145/ 3.89	2850	46.3/53.7

we put on our driving gloves and set out for fun in this group of three, the last guy to grab gets the SLK keys. The automatic transmission is part of the problem. Why turn over to automation one of the fun parts of driving? The supercharged four-cylinder is not quite aesthetically pleasing, either. The *putt-putt-putt* exhaust sound at idle is too close to a Farmall's, and power flow tends toward an abrupt on/off, depending on accelerator position and the automatic's inclination toward gear-changes. Too many important decisions are taken away from the driver and relegated to HAL or whatever silicon pseudonym is on duty.

We don't love the handling, either, an assertion that surely requires some explanation since the Test Results panel gives the SLK top marks for cornering and braking grip—0.90 g on the skidpad and 170 feet to stop from 70 mph. The problem here is attitude. The SLK is secretive. Virtually no information comes back through the steering. Imagine a rheostat for dialing up cornering forces. Turn the wheel more; cornering force goes up. As for a sense of what the tires are doing, the steering answers, "What tires?" Experienced drivers, either consciously or unconsciously, rely on subtle changes in tire-slip angle to know where they're operating relative to the limits of the tires. Slip angles increase as cornering forces rise, and the increase goes nonlinear when you near the limit. Feeling for this nonlinearity enables you to drive on the edge without ever falling off. But this car gives no sense of the edge. Don Schroeder, who drove the track portion of the test, reports that the SLK's remarkably high lane-change speed—more than 4 mph better than the others'—was achieved with no sense of the tires slipping. And when slipping finally becomes apparent, "you encounter a spooky handling abyss," he says.

Of course, this abyss shows itself only at extremely high lateral forces, and one can usually keep up with the other cars in this test with little risk. But sports-car fun comes more from control than from speed, and the joy of controlling this machine is largely absent.

Truth to tell, when we think of sports

emergency lane-change maneuver, mph	interior sound level, dBA				fuel economy, mpg		
	idle	full throttle	70-mph cruising	70-mph coasting	EPA city	EPA highway	C/D 500-mile trip
61.7	51	77	77	76	19	27	19
66.3	46	77	74	74	22	30	21
61.9	55	86	76	75	19	27	20
63.3	51	80	76	75	20	28	20

dimensions, inches				fuel tank, gallons	interior volume, cubic feet		suspension		brakes, front/rear	tires
wheel-base	length	width	height		front	trunk	front	rear		
96.3	158.5	66.6	50.7	13.5	47	5	ind, strut located by a control arm, coil springs, anti-roll bar	ind, semi-trailing arms, coil springs, anti-roll bar	vented disc/disc; anti-lock control	Michelin Pilot HX, 225/50ZR-16
94.5	157.3	67.5	50.8	14.0	48	10/4 (top up/down)	ind, unequal-length control arms, coil springs, anti-roll bar	ind; 3 lateral links, 1 diagonal link, and 1 toe-control link per side; coil springs; anti-roll bar	vented disc/disc; anti-lock control	Michelin Pilot HX; F: 205/55VR-16, R: 225/50VR-16
95.2	171.0	70.1	50.8	15.3	47	9	ind, strut located by a control arm, coil springs, anti-roll bar	ind, strut located by 1 trailing and 2 lateral links, coil springs, anti-roll bar	vented disc/vented disc; anti-lock control	Bridgestone Potenza S-02; F: 205/55ZR-16, R: 225/50ZR-16

cars, we never think of the vastly more expensive Mercedes SL two-seaters, either. The SLK shares with the SL line a family resemblance long on solid construction, comfortable appointments, serious engine power, and enduring styling. But none of these cars spreads grins across the faces of sports-car guys.

The SLK's acceleration times are slightly behind the others' here, largely because of the automatic. Zero to 60 takes 7.2 seconds, and the quarter-mile slips past in 15.5 seconds at 91 mph. On our comparison trip, the SLK outscored the others in fuel economy at 21 mpg, compared with 20 for the Porsche and 19 for the BMW. And on cold mornings, the heater of this SLK blew out plenty of BTUs, unlike the last one we tested.

Whereas we're firm in our conviction that the SLK comes up short as a sports car, we're also aware that the majority of wanna-owns prefer it that way.

Second Place
BMW Z3 2.8

Maybe this runabout can't restore departing hair or shrink the bags under the eyes, but it sure brings to mind our younger days and the Triumph TR6. The snorty 2.8-liter six makes the same textural growl (though greatly muted compared with that old Brit), the narrow-at-the-elbows cockpit positions the torso upright behind the wheel, the long hood sweeps across the view as we turn, the rear suspension responds to power with that familiar demi-squat.

Good stuff? Wrong question. The Z3 delivers that rare car flavor, one that's been savored since Morgans were young, sought after by drivers who shun decaf and power steering with equal vigor. The flavor here is *sports car*, hot and black.

In fact, the Z3 has power steering and power brakes and power windows and a power up/down adjuster on the driver's seat—all niceties that have watered down the hearty flavor of sports cars over the past several decades. This is by no means the snow-in-the-cockpit experience that Triumph-MG-Healey drivers welcomed as proof that they were apart from the crowd of sedan-slogging wienies.

And yet—is this a time machine hauling us back to the '60s?—the Z3's windshield shakes on bumpy roads, air currents roil into the cockpit from *behind*, the stubby gear lever pokes up out of a tall tunnel that might just as well be the Continental Divide for the way it separates the cockpit into two sides. And there goes the rear again, hunkering down as the clutch takes up.

No question that this Z3 is closer to the traditional sports-car definition than anything else in stores these days (the Miata excepted, of course).

New for 1997 is this six-cylinder version, the extra 51 horsepower accompanied by vented front brakes (the same diameter as on the four), a rear track increased by 2.5 inches, a limited-slip differential, and a new front spoiler.

The torque starts low in the rev range and pours on smoothly and sweetly as the tach swings upward. This is a disciplined powertrain, never raucous. It propels the Z3 to 60 mph in 6.3 seconds, 1.8 seconds quicker than the four-cylinder Z3, and just a tick behind the quickest of this group, the Porsche. Top speed is governor-limited at 129 mph.

Unlike the SLK, there's lots of communication here. The cockpit feels close, more intimate than the others. You're in touch. You have a sense of what the machinery is doing. The steering feels substan-

BMW Z3 2.8

Highs: Smooth power from the six, amusing handling from the semi-trailing-arm rear, convincing sports-car mood in the cockpit.

Lows: "Amusing handling" isn't the same as correct handling, skimpy features list makes price seem steep (unless you value high-visibility BMW circle logos).

The Verdict: Very much a traditional sports car, with all the joys and gripes that entails.

Porsche Boxster

Highs: Two trunks, a power roof, slick moves in the twisties, and just enough traditional Porsche cues to remind that this company always does its own thing.

Lows: No engine access from the top? Is this an annuity for the dealer mechanics, or what?

The Verdict: Thoroughly fun to drive, thoroughly unconventional, thoroughly Porsche.

tial—"meaty" in the words of one of our testers. You can grab hold of it. Road adhesion is about medium for this group at 0.87 g. Handling is exactly what you'd expect of a front-engine car with semi-trailing arms behind: predictable understeer. Yet lifting abruptly off the power in turns will step the rear out to heroic drift angles, even at relatively low lateral forces. Controlling same is easy and intuitive, however.

With the top down and the side windows up, we rushed along some high desert roads at speeds up to 110 mph. Drafty, yes, but not so much so that it wasn't fun, never mind that temperatures were in the 50s. Sports cars goad you into bursts of exuberance like that. With the top up, this car has considerably more windrush noise than the others.

Downing the Z3's top is a do-it-yourself project bereft of power assists—unlatch the header, push back till the stack drops into the well behind the seat, and then the cover, stored in the trunk, must be snapped into place. The details are well designed and simple. One of our staffers, by himself, did the job in 54 seconds.

Still, the *manual* top, along with a short roll call of features, a plainly appointed black cockpit, and the list of conventional BMW-sedan mechanicals under the skin, says that the Z3 is a rather short reach for its maker—certainly a far less imaginative concept than either the SLK or the Boxster. Yes, our as-tested car lists for about four large less than the others

here, but the Z3 seems fully priced to us.

First Place
Porsche Boxster

"Nosy" is the visual first impression of this car—the nose Pinocchios out in front of the wheels an astonishing distance. Let it be your warning that the Boxster does nothing the ordinary way.

We give it top marks in this group because it drives superbly and plies us with creature comforts to boot. It's a bold rethink of how a sports car might be configured—the long nose makes room for two radiators, one ahead of each front wheel. The rethink is incautious, too. All engine work—hell, all peaking into the engine room—must be done from the bottom. The trunk opens to reveal a corner devoted to service: dipstick, oil and coolant fillers. That's the *rear* trunk. The *front* trunk gives access to brake fluid and washer juice. The engine itself?

Well, they *say* it's in that box behind the seats.

Wherever it is, it's a sweet contributor to this car's success. It makes whirring sounds, quite loud and clatter-free in a way foreign to Porsches. These whirs fade to background when you're driving. The cockpit is serene. Unless the top is down. Then, if the road is right, you hear organ-pipe resonances more beautiful than any since Bach when the intake and exhaust passages pass through their 5200-to-5500-rpm tuned frequencies as the flat-six rushes toward 201 hp at 6000 rpm.

The rush delivers 60 mph from rest in 6.2 seconds, and finishes the quarter-mile in 14.8 seconds at 93 mph, quickest of this group. Drat! The Boxster, in the lower gears, passes too quickly through its tuned peaks to even notice them. But the music that accompanies the labored acceleration up mountain grades is worth however many vacation days a flatlander's journey may take.

While in the mountains, enjoy the switchbacks. The Boxster's cornering behavior is first-rate. The steering stays lively and responsive at the limit, and the rear tracks reliably behind. Porsche brags of a new way of managing deflection steer in the rear wheels. It works. This is not a tail-happy handler, never mind the reputation of mid-engine cars. The low-profile Bridgestone Potenza S-02 tires deserve mention here. Their dramatic gatorback tread pattern is almost as notable as the Boxster's nosy profile. Their grip is surprisingly low, a disappointing 0.81 g on

the skidpad, by far less tenacious than the other cars' Michelins. But their breakaway characteristics are wonderfully gradual, so the Boxster is easily controllable and steerable at the limit. We repeat: Control is the fun of a sports car, and if you have it, you can often outrun cars that produce better numbers in highly practiced test-track maneuvers. Would the SLK be more fun on these tires, we wonder?

In sharp contrast to the Z3's traditional approach, the Boxster seems devoid of all tradition save the occasional Porsche touch (the single, center-outlet exhaust reminds of so many 356 racers). The body is round-shouldered, the cockpit is wide, the instruments are marked in italic typefaces, plastic interior details are *shiny* black—this from the company that, in the early Seventies, originated the fashion of flat-black trim instead of chrome.

Porsche's rethink of the sports car shows in the power top, too. A single latch at the top of the windshield must be freed by hand. Then one button stows the roof under a hatch at the rear of the cockpit in just 12 seconds, less than half the time of the next-best Mercedes. Well, it *almost* stows the roof: A moon-shaped section of it remains visible behind the twin roll bars, a packaging necessity turned into an audacious design element.

Audacious describes the whole package. And fun. We expect that a rethink this radical, from a maker of such low volume, will devil early owners with a few bothers. Ah, but Boxster mechanicals come with a two-year unlimited-mileage warranty, something you could never say for springtime love. ●

It Was the Shape of Things to Come. And It Came and Went.

With so much publicity surrounding the new German roadsters, you might conclude that fast, modestly priced European roadsters are something new in the States. But as few as 16 years ago, a very similar car was available to U.S. car buyers—the Triumph TR8, a British sports car.

There are interesting similarities. Like the Z3 2.8, the TR8 played big brother to a four-cylinder car (the TR7). In this case, the engine swap was for an aluminum Buick-Rover 3.5-liter V-8. Its layout—two seats with a usable trunk—matches the German roadsters', as does its suspension tuning, aimed at balancing ride comfort and handling. At $11,900, the 1980 TR8 ragtop cost about as much as a Corvette coupe—as is the case with these new roadsters.

The TR8's performance falls short of these newer cars, but not by a mile. In August 1980, we coaxed 0-to-60-mph times of 8.1 seconds and a quarter-mile of 16.2 seconds out of a five-speed fuel-injected 137-horsepower TR8. We found the steering "surprisingly sensitive and pleasant." The only disappointment was the brakes, with 70-to-0-mph stops taking a long 228 feet. Still, a slick droptop with this performance was electrifying news in 1980. We called the TR8 "nothing less than

the reinvention of the sports car."

Owning a nicely restored TR8 affords yours truly a modern perspective. Even today, the TR8 is a charming drive, with good power, balanced handling, a comfortable cockpit, and a healthy dollop of character right down to its plaid seat fabric. And its styling has aged better than most cars' of the era. On the other hand, the TR8's less-than-tight structure, marginal brakes, and solid-axle rear suspension would not be acceptable to today's car buyers. The TR8 might be nearly as fun to drive as the newcomers, but as for refinement—there's no contest.

Triumph built about 2500 TR8 coupes and convertibles before the marque succumbed to British Leyland's inept management in 1981. Today, TR8s in nice shape can be found for $5000 to $10,000. —*Don Schroeder*

		engine	trans-mission	brakes	handling	ride	driver comfort	ergo-nomics	features and amenities	value	styling	fun to drive	design clever-ness	OVERALL RATING*
Editors' Ratings	BMW Z3 2.8	8	8	8	8	8	8	8	6	8	8	9	7	92
	MERCEDES-BENZ SLK	7	7	8	7	8	8	9	10	9	9	8	9	91
	PORSCHE BOXSTER	9	9	9	9	8	9	9	8	8	9	9	9	95

HOW IT WORKS: Editors rate vehicles from 1 to 10 (10 being best) in each category, then scores are collected and averaged, resulting in the numbers shown above.

*The overall rating is not the total of these numbers. Rather, it is an independent judgment (on a 1-to-100 scale) that includes other factors—even personal preferences—not easily categorized.

1956 meets 2001.

Presenting the Boxster. It's classic, yet futuristic. It's a cross between a 550 Spyder and the space shuttle.

It's the first mid-engine Porsche roadster in over 40 years. And it's in the Here and Now.

Starting at $39,980. Contact us at 1-800-PORSCHE or http://www.porsche-usa.com and come to believe:

Porsche. There is no substitute.℠

We like numbers. Numbers are our friends. Numbers sing arias of irrefutable fact that soar above murky choruses of subjectivity, spin, and slant. Numbers can baby-sit our kids anytime.

So wrap your wetware around this number: 5724—as in pounds, as in curb weight for the Porsche Cayenne Turbo. This is almost exactly the weight of a GMC Yukon XL—a perimeter-frame four-by-four truck with a 12,000-pound towing capacity and 17.6 more inches of wheelbase than the unit-bodied Cayenne Turbo. This number—the weight of our test vehicle with all the fluids onboard—is approximately one Harley-Davidson Sportster more than we expected the Cayenne Turbo to weigh, based on the company's specifications. Around the office, many a jaw has gone oafishly slack at this imposing avoirdupois—and the jaw-slacking bar is set pretty high here.

Our scales, meanwhile, have quit to find easier work in the piano-moving business.

This number goes to the heart of the Cayenne conundrum: Why, when a statistically insignificant number of SUV owners ever venture off-road, would Porsche—a company that year in, year out builds the best sports cars in the world—burden the Cayenne with such silly amounts of heavy, hillock-humping capacity? Twenty-two-inch fording depth? More than 10 inches of ground clearance, courtesy of a ride-height-adjustable air suspension? A torque-multiplying low-range gear ratio and locking center and rear differentials?

This is not to quarrel with Porsche CEO Wendelin Wiedeking's decision, in 1998, to stick a Porsche-badged snout in the SUV trough. Nor is it to diminish, exactly, the Cayenne T's off-road abilities, which include leaping over felled trees in a single bound (it has an approach angle of 32.4 degrees and a departure angle of 27.3 degrees). But after 600 miles of mixed driving in the Cayenne Turbo—from *Vanishing Point*–style transits of upper Lower Michigan to plowing through dirty, smelly filth holes (the *restaurants* of upper Lower)—we have reached the conclusion that rather than digitally morph a Range Rover with a 911 Turbo, Porsche has created a vehicle that feels like a superb all-wheel-drive tourer with an elephant on its back.

Is it fast? Is Wiedeking hard to spell? The vehicle's quickness and speed (we recorded 0 to 60 mph in 5.0 seconds and a quarter-mile pass in 13.5 seconds) are stunning, but here numbers fail us; it's not the velocity per se but the giddy sensation of enormous mass being manhandled by oceanic force, like a tugboat thrown on the beach by a tsunami. The Cayenne reactor is a twin-turbo, quad-cam 4.5-liter V-8 with dry-sump and other fancy plumbing to keep it oily and cool in extreme off-roading. Thanks to its VarioCam intake-valve timing, the motor produces peak torque of 457 pound-feet between 2250 and 4750 rpm and a nice fat 450 horsepower at 6000 rpm. The soundtrack to all of this is a futuristic warbling of metallic timbre and menacing vibrato that makes *The Matrix* soundtrack seem like folk music.

An Aisin-supplied six-speed automatic transmission with Tiptronic override converts engine speed to driveshaft rotation with shaved-leg

ROAD TEST

Porsche Cayenne Turbo

We weigh the Porsche against other SUVs and give ourselves a hernia.

BY DAN NEIL

smoothness. Downstream of that is a planetary center differential that normally sends 62 percent of the go juice to the rear wheels, but using a multiplate clutch, the Porsche Traction Management system can shunt up to 100 percent of engine torque to whichever axle needs it.

Around-town driving is supremely civilized, with finely modulated throttle tip-in and stop-and-go manners. But when you summon the full 8.7 psi of turbo pressure to pass on a country road—*Oy vay!*—the Tiptronic executes a nifty double kickdown and the vehicle squirts like hot Cheez Whiz. In the time it takes to swallow hard, the Cayenne Turbo is well into civil-aviation speeds.

Wow. Imagine what it would be like if it weighed 1000 pounds less!

If you are so bourgeois as to consider the tedious *value* formula, the smashmouth Turbo we tested was $94,980 (with optional niceties such as a sunroof, a CD changer, and keyless entry). The Cayenne S—the non-turbocharged version propelled by a relatively noodle-armed 340

COUNTERPOINT

After exercising this rig on a number of road-racing circuits during the 2003 One Lap of America run, I can confidently say the Cayenne is a lovely highway ride. I can say even more confidently that it is *not* at home on a racetrack, particularly one with lots of linked turns and decreasing radii. We are talking dynamic reluctance on a vast scale here. A goal was to give it Porsche-sports-car virtues to go with its superb off-road capabilities. But that just ain't compatible with a vehicle weighing almost three tons. I suppose you can teach an elephant to be a sprinter, but why not start with a gazelle? *—Tony Swan*

Listen up, all you nouveau-riche rappers and cash-phat NBA power forwards who are right now trading in your G-wagens for this even-more-expensive superstatus symbol: You can get stuck in the mud in this *wunder*truck (see left) very easily with these Pirellis, which are designed for the highway. That happened in rural Michigan last spring, when one of us

decided to drive through a farmer's soggy field. The expensive 19-inch P Zeros sank right up to the hubs. It was a plain ol' pickup truck that pulled this 450-hp technological marvel from the muck. Reminds us of all the SUV owners we saw in ditches last winter who thought their SUVs made them invincible. *—Steve Spence*

It's hard to believe a vehicle this heavy can be thrust forward this quickly with a mere 450 turbocharged horsepower, but the numbers don't lie. The Cayenne is seriously quick, and capable of 161 mph, which puts it in a category all by itself. It's also a demon off-road, as I found out during the course of running in the Cayenne Crossing Drive for Hope, a cross-country charity run using two-lane and no-lane roads on a 2700-mile course. On the Peter's Mill trail in northern Virginia, the Cayenne Turbo just reared back and laughed at the rocky terrain, lifted itself up off the suspension, and handily went through eight miles of pure hell. *—Jim McCraw*

horsepower and 310 pound-feet of torque—starts at $56,665 and can be optioned to more than $80,000.

As you might expect, it takes an extraordinary exertion of technology to achieve excellent handling with this much mass while still retaining ride comfort. The suspension is a Byzantine hybrid of control arms attached to tubular and plate steel subframes, with all four corners sitting on air springs assisted by adaptive dampers that can be set in comfort, normal, and sport modes. Vehicle ride height lowers as speeds increase (a full 1.5 inches lower than normal at speeds above 130 mph), and the damper stiffness defaults to sport mode if the vehicle's accelerometers detect more than the usual thrashing about. Porsche Stability Management wrangles the antilock-brake, brake-force-distribution, ride-

leveling, and all-wheel-drive traction-control systems to keep the Cayenne upright and on course. As a result of these interventions, the Cayenne's dynamics have a peculiar, synthetic feel to them; it sometimes feels as if the faster you go in the Cayenne, the flatter it corners.

Yet with the damper control set on sport and the ride height on low, the Cayenne arcs around a highway on-ramp with a nice, edgy tautness. The rear end does an ever-so-slight hip shift on initial turn-in, characteristic of recent Porsches, and then hunkers down in a composed four-wheel drift. If the ramp tightens and you need to get out of the throttle, it's okay. The Cayenne, like the 911, does only the slightest wiggle before the rear toe-in tightens up and the tail tucks in.

Yet for all the sensors, processors,

adaptive kinematics, and the like—to say nothing of the optional 19-inch Pirelli P Zero Rossos—the Cayenne generates only decent cornering grip, 0.82 g on the skidpad, a number handily exceeded by an Infiniti FX45, for one. Shove the vehicle around, and you'll soon wish you had more tire under you. The feeling is a little like driving on bias-ply tires.

The Cayenne's weight dampens our enthusiasm in other ways. The braking distance from 70 mph, 170 feet, is six feet longer than a BMW X5 4.6is's—this despite the fact the Cayenne has six-piston front calipers and gigantic vented discs. And according to fearless leader Tony Swan, this same sport-ute's brakes got a little squishy during his intrepid One Lap flog-fest (see story on page 142). How very un-Porschelike.

Make no mistake: The Cayenne Turbo is an extraordinary machine, beautifully crafted, sumptuously provisioned, modestly—*ahem*—styled. It is the fastest production SUV on the planet, and it has more off-road chops than Sir Edmund Hillary. It's sure to be a huge status codpiece in South Beach and Beverly Hills. It is the "Porsche of SUVs." We had hoped for a little more Porsche and a little less SUV. •

C/D TEST RESULTS

ACCELERATION

	Seconds
Zero to 30 mph	1.7
40 mph	2.8
50 mph	3.8
60 mph	5.0
70 mph	6.8
80 mph	8.6
90 mph	10.5
100 mph	13.0
110 mph	16.0
120 mph	19.6
130 mph	24.8
140 mph	32.6
Street start, 5–60 mph	6.1
Top-gear acceleration, 30–50 mph	2.8
50–70 mph	3.6
Standing ¼-mile	13.5 sec @ 104 mph
Top speed (drag limited)	161 mph

BRAKING
70–0 mph @ impending lockup ....170 ft
Fade ....none **light** moderate heavy

HANDLING
Roadholding, 300-ft-dia skidpad ....0.82 g
Understeer ....**minimal** moderate excessive

FUEL ECONOMY
EPA city driving ....13 mpg
EPA highway driving ....18 mpg
C/D-observed ....**12 mpg**

INTERIOR SOUND LEVEL
Idle ....43 dBA
Full-throttle acceleration ....72 dBA
70-mph cruising ....67 dBA

PORSCHE CAYENNE TURBO
Vehicle type: front-engine, 4-wheel-drive, 5-passenger, 5-door wagon

Price as tested: $94,980

Price and option breakdown: base Porsche Cayenne Turbo (includes $765 freight), $89,665; sunroof, $1100; keyless-entry system, $995; Electric Comfort package (includes power tailgate latch, self-dimming mirrors, and integrated garage-door opener), $890; 19-inch wheels and performance tires, $850; in-dash 6-CD changer, $715; trailer hitch, $590; logo wheel hub covers, $175

Major standard accessories: power steering, windows, seats, and locks; A/C; cruise control; tilting and telescoping steering wheel; rear defroster and wiper

Sound system: Bose AM/FM-stereo radio/CD changer, 13 speakers

ENGINE
Type ....twin-turbocharged and intercooled V-8, aluminum block and heads
Bore x stroke ....3.66 x 3.27 in, 93.0 x 83.0mm
Displacement ....275 cu in, 4510cc
Compression ratio 9.5:1
Engine-control system ....Bosch Motronic ME7.1.1 with port fuel injection
Emissions controls ......3-way catalytic converter, feedback air-fuel-ratio control
Turbochargers ....2, KKK
Waste gate ....integral
Maximum boost pressure ....8.7 psi
Valve gear ....chain-driven double overhead cams, 4 valves per cylinder, hydraulic lifters, variable intake-valve timing
Power (SAE net) ....450 bhp @ 6000 rpm
Torque (SAE net) ....457 lb-ft @ 2250 rpm
Redline ....6400 rpm

DRIVETRAIN
Transmission ....6-speed automatic with lockup torque converter
Final-drive ratio ....3.70:1, limited slip
Transfer-gear ratios ....L, 2.71:1; H, 1.00:1

Gear	Ratio	Mph/1000 rpm (L/H)	Max. test speed (L/H)
I	4.15	2.0/5.4	13/34 mph (6400/6400 rpm)
II	2.37	3.5/9.4	22/60 mph (6400/6400 rpm)
III	1.56	5.3/14.3	34/92 mph (6400/6400 rpm)
IV	1.16	7.1/19.2	45/123 mph (6400/6400 rpm)
V	0.86	9.6/25.9	61/161 mph (6400/6200 rpm)
VI	0.69	11.9/32.2	76/161 mph (6400/5000 rpm)

DIMENSIONS AND CAPACITIES
Wheelbase ....112.4 in
Track, F/R ....64.6/65.2 in
Length ....188.3 in
Width ....75.9 in

Height ....66.9 in
Ground clearance ....6.2–10.0 in
Curb weight ....5724 lb
Weight distribution, F/R 52.9/47.1%
Fuel capacity ....26.4 gal
Oil capacity ....8.9 qt
Water capacity ....10.6 qt

CHASSIS/BODY
Type ....unit construction with a subframe
Body material ....welded steel stampings

INTERIOR
SAE volume, front seat ....57 cu ft
rear seat ....49 cu ft
cargo volume, seats up/down ......19/63 cu ft
Practical cargo room, length of pipe ....128.0 in
largest sheet of plywood ....61.0 x 45.5 in
no. of 10 x 10 x 16-in boxes, seats in/out 14/28
Front seats ....bucket
Seat adjustments ...fore and aft, seatback angle, front height, rear height, lumbar support
Restraint systems, front ......manual 3-point belts; driver and passenger front, side, and curtain airbags
rear ....manual 3-point belts, outboard curtain airbags
General comfort ....poor fair **good** excellent
Fore-and-aft support ....poor fair good **excellent**
Lateral support ....poor **fair** good excellent

SUSPENSION
F: ....ind; unequal-length control arms; 6-position height-adjustable, self-leveling air springs; 3-position cockpit-adjustable, electronically controlled shock absorbers; hydraulically engaged anti-roll bar
R: ......ind; 1 control arm, 1 lateral link, 1 diagonal link, and 1 toe-control link per side; 6-position height-adjustable, self-leveling air springs; 3-position cockpit-adjustable, electronically controlled shock absorbers; hydraulically engaged anti-roll bar

STEERING
Type ....rack-and-pinion, power-assisted
Turns lock-to-lock 2.7
Turning circle curb-to-curb ....39.0 ft

BRAKES
F: ....13.8 x 1.3-in vented disc
R: ....13.0 x 1.1-in vented disc
Power assist ....vacuum with anti-lock control

WHEELS AND TIRES
Wheel size ....9.0 x 19 in
Wheel type ....cast aluminum
Tires ....Pirelli P Zero Rosso, 275/45ZR-19 108Y
Test inflation pressures, F/R ....38/42 psi

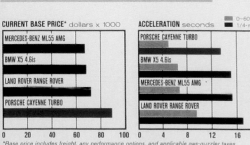

CURRENT BASE PRICE* dollars x 1000
Mercedes-Benz ML55 AMG
BMW X5 4.6is
Land Rover Range Rover
Porsche Cayenne Turbo
0 20 40 60 80 100
*Base price includes freight, any performance options, and applicable gas-guzzler taxes.

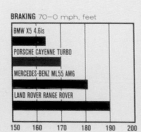

ACCELERATION seconds 0–60 mph / ¼-mile
Porsche Cayenne Turbo
BMW X5 4.6is
Mercedes-Benz ML55 AMG
Land Rover Range Rover
0 4 8 12 16 20

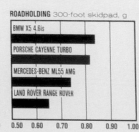

BRAKING 70–0 mph, feet
BMW X5 4.6is
Porsche Cayenne Turbo
Mercedes-Benz ML55 AMG
Land Rover Range Rover
150 160 170 180 190 200

ROADHOLDING 300-foot skidpad, g
BMW X5 4.6is
Porsche Cayenne Turbo
Mercedes-Benz ML55 AMG
Land Rover Range Rover
0.50 0.60 0.70 0.80 0.90 1.00

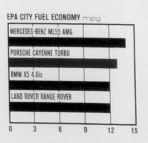

EPA CITY FUEL ECONOMY mpg
Mercedes-Benz ML55 AMG
Porsche Cayenne Turbo
BMW X5 4.6is
Land Rover Range Rover
0 3 6 9 12 15

Do you really need 450 hp to pick up diapers? You ever run out of diapers?

The Qwikie Mart doesn't get any quickier. Cayenne Turbo. Seamless acceleration through all six gears. 0 to 60 in 5.2 seconds. The stability of Porsche Traction Management and Active Suspension. An SUV, but decidedly a Porsche when you need one most. Porsche. There is no substitute.

The Cayenne Turbo

PREVIEW PORSCHE CARRERA GT

Why everything else amounts to toothbrushes and coffee machines.

BY DANIEL PUND

It's not the $440,000 Carrera GT's absurdly fast top speed that awes you—we were aboard yet had no fear as Porsche's test driver clocked 208 mph (with a tailwind) on a Soviet-era military runway in the former East Germany.

It's not this Ferrari Enzo fighter's equally absurd accelerative force, either: Porsche modestly claims a 0-to-62-mph time of 3.9 seconds, but it's probably more like 3.5 seconds.

It's not even the otherworldly strength of the gigantic ceramic brakes that made the greatest impression on us, although they are strong enough at full clamp to lift the passenger fully

away from his leather-covered, carbon-Kevlar seat and hard against the locked seatbelt.

No question—all these feats are stratospherically impressive. But they are just extensions of what you've felt before in a common automobile. These figures don't reveal the character of the Carrera GT any more than one's familiarity with hops, barley, and water explains how they can make you drunk.

Porsche says it will build 1500 of these supercars over the next three years. The Carrera GT, which began life as a proposal for a Le Mans race car, is nothing if not uncommon. In truth, it's not even a car, really. It's not like those

things we put in comparison tests and rate the ergonomics and measure the gas mileage of—all those conveyances that operate in the vast gray center of the performance spectrum. The 604-hp Carrera GT is different. It's all vibrancy and immediacy.

It was actually turning off the ignition after our brief initial drive that first amazed us. The millisecond the ignition circuit is broken, there is . . . *nothing*. Normally, when you key the ignition off, the crankshaft makes a few extra lazy rotations as the mass of the moving parts takes a half-beat to submit to friction and come to a complete rest. It's a universal experience we

take for granted.

But in the GT, the crankshaft stops with a new suddenness—immediately, now, before your brain even considers the causal relationship between turning the key and the engine coming to rest. It's as if the crankshaft had seized within a quarter-rotation after the last spark plug fired. There is no mass at all to speak of in the drivetrain. Take, for example, the lightweight ceramic clutch (measuring a mere 6.7 inches in diameter) and the 10 titanium connecting rods in this 68-degree V-10. They weigh, by regular commodity-car standards, essentially nothing. After a romp in the GT, whatever you drive will feel

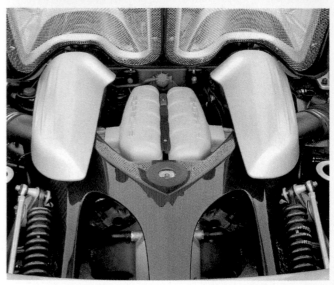

as if it were powered by a huge diesel—the kind we imagine powering ocean liners—with 10-foot-long iron connecting rods.

This works, of course, in reverse, too. Unlike the brawny powerplant of, say, a Lamborghini Murciélago or Dodge Viper, which pummels physics into submission, the Porsche's race-bred V-10 seems to skirt physics entirely. It always feels unrestrained. Here again we can thank low rotational mass. The best production-car engines in the world accumulate revs in a satisfyingly smooth sweep. So quick to rev is the 5.7-liter Porsche engine that you scarcely are aware that it's putting forth any effort at all. A stab of the wide, floor-mounted gas pedal and—*Brip!*—you're at the 8000-rpm power peak. Watch the in-car footage of an F1 car going up through the gears with its brief, staccato blasts through the revs, then slow the footage down by about half, and you get the idea.

This audiovisual trick will also roughly approximate the sound the GT makes. It's similar in timbre to an F1 motor but brawnier because of its greater displacement. Its note is a register lower because it runs fewer revs, and of course, it won't pierce your eardrums—there's a muffler. There is no time to adjust your mind-set between the docility of idle and the full-on, screaming fury of redline. Holy crap! Not even the standard traction-control system can keep up.

The downside to this is that you will stall the car from a standstill. Everyone who sat in the driver's seat did. Well, you'll either stall it, or your big dumb right foot will call for far too many revs, spin the rear tires furiously, and a second later get shut down by traction control. This display of skill and precision doesn't impress the assembled Porsche personnel as much as you might imagine. Your best bet is to gingerly ease out the clutch pedal and keep your foot off the hair-trigger throttle. As the clutch hooks up, the idle automatically rises to about 1800 rpm, and you inch away—slowly, but with your dignity intact.

Once under way, you'll notice, perhaps for the first time in your life if you're of the male persuasion, that you have breasts. You may prefer to think of them as "pectorals at rest." Whatever, they're there, and they're moving violently in sympathy to each road dip and hillock. Meanwhile, nothing else in the car is moving. The Carrera GT is topless (with two removable carbon-fiber roof panels), yet there is no movement, no creak, no nothing going on in the carbon-fiber structure. The suspension—unequal-length control arms all around with race-car-style, pushrod-activated coil-overs mounted to the structure—will yield very little to a lowly road undulation, and because the structure will not bend even to the degree

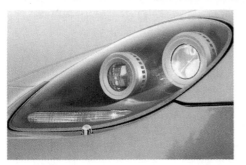

at-the-limit behavior on a slalom course. Still, the concrete surface we tried this on had about the same coefficient of friction as 80-grit sandpaper, so turn-in was shockingly immediate and the GT constantly suggested rotating around its engine—but it never spun out. There is zero body roll (possibly you may have expected that). The Carrera GT offers no electronic stability-control system because, as Porsche explains, "the driving behavior is very good, and there is, therefore, no need for it." Theoretically, this is true. Unfortunately, at issue is the driving behavior of the pilot. For instance, we'd bet that the French reporter who ran a GT into an unmoving roadside object at considerable speed might have found ESP quite helpful.

Neither does the Carrera GT have a robotized clutch-pedal-less shifting system, like that in the Ferrari Enzo. Mounted high on the tall center console is a traditional dogleg shifter. Porsche contends that none of the paddle-shifting systems currently on the market is good enough for its baby. And we agree. Besides, matching your own revs on downshifts and smoothing upshifts with a judicious left foot are ultimately more involving than Ferrari's system. The one advantage of such systems, though, is they will not allow the driver to overrev the motor as one writer did with an ill-advised fifth-to-second downshift, lunching the hyper-expensive motor in one brief, but eternally regrettable, error.

There are other downsides to driving a GT1 racer on public roads, such as scuffing, as we did, the carbon-fiber bottom on a routine bump. You'll also want to be aware that the hind end of your GT is 75.6 inches wide (a fraction of an inch narrower than a Lincoln Aviator). Place it carefully.

But these are such plebeian concerns. We have been to the top of the mountain, and we're ruined for such trivialities. ∎

that stiff steel or aluminum cars will, all the movement is transferred to your unrestrained body bits. Unlike that of many super sports cars, or even mere sports cars, though, the Carrera GT's ride is not harsh. It doesn't feel nervous or skittish on imperfect roads. And unlike other fat-tired sports cars (the Porsche wears 265/35ZR-19 Michelins up front and 335/30ZR-20s in back), the GT doesn't suffer from bump steer. Truck troughs and crowned roads are beneath its consideration.

Curiously, the Carrera's handling character is determined to an unusual degree by the powertrain as well. When designing a thing as spectacularly impractical as the GT, engineers can obsessively focus on achieving a low—nearly subterranean—center of gravity. The GT's crankshaft spins just 3.9 inches above its carbon-fiber floor. This is made possible by the engine's dry-sump oiling system and that small-diameter clutch. The six-speed transmission actually sits lower in the car than the differential. Only a fool, or a select few automotive writers, would explore the handling limits of this thing on public roads. We chose instead to gather what we could about the GT's

PORSCHE CARRERA GT
Vehicle type: mid-engine, rear-wheel-drive, 2-passenger, 2-door Targa
Estimated base price: $440,000
Engine type: DOHC 40-valve V-10, aluminum block and heads, port fuel injection
Displacement . . . . .350 cu in, 5733cc
Power (SAE net) . . . . .604 bhp @ 8000 rpm
Torque (SAE net) . . . . .435 lb-ft @ 5750 rpm

Transmission	6-speed manual
Wheelbase	107.5 in
Length/width/height	181.6/75.6/45.9 in
Curb weight	3050 lb

Manufacturer's performance ratings:
Zero to 62 mph . . . . .3.9 sec
Zero to 124 mph . . . . .9.9 sec
Top speed (drag limited) . . . . .205 mph
Projected fuel economy:
European urban cycle . . . . .8 mpg
extra-urban cycle . . . . .20 mpg
combined cycle . . . . .13 mpg

ROAD TEST PORSCHE 911 CARRERA S

Porsche returns some things that were lost.

BY AARON ROBINSON

PHOTOGRAPHY BY AARON KILEY

Where does the Porsche 911 go from here? It's a fair question, considering this is the 97th article this magazine has published since 1965 about roadgoing 911s.

We've spun out in all the variants from the 912 to the shovel-nosed 930. We've twisted driveshafts in all the Carrera 4s. We've compared 911s to everything from Corvettes to De Loreans to motorcycles to airplanes. The best line ever published about a Porsche was in this very magazine in 1980, when P.J. O'Rourke called it an "ass-engine Nazi slot car."

So here, in story No. 97, a road test of the new "997" model, we gotta ask,

"What's next?" This 2005 Porsche 911 Carrera S—the S denoting a 29-horsepower, $9800 upgrade over the base $70,065 rear-drive Carrera, or a breathtaking $85,910, as optioned here—is the best Carrera Porsche has ever built. The company achieved that partly through new technology but mainly by reversing the car back to better days of styling and attitude. If backward is better, has the 911 hit an evolutionary dead end?

The outgoing Porsche 911, code-named the 996 (see stories 65 through 95), was supposed to be the best; faster, quieter, cleaner, more flexible, better built—the Swabian summit of ass-engine

engineering. Launched in 1998, that first water-cooled 911 was all those things and a delight to drive. Both lap times and warranty items dropped with the 996 we drove over a 40,000-mile test, but the car just wasn't as fun as its frisky air-cooled predecessor. Many here considered the 996 colder, duller, more remote, and cheaper inside. It had less Porsche passion and more Toyota calculation. A team of retired Toyota execs was consulting for Porsche at the time of the 996's incubation. Coincidence?

Consider that of five comparison tests to which we subjected the 996, the Porsche lost all save one, where it was pitted against unworthy opponents: a Jaguar XKR and a Panoz Esperante. Porsche had modernized its derriere-engined darling right into a box, and the only way out, at least in some respects, was backward, with the return of a few Porsche 911 peculiarities that were lost in the last go-round.

Among the lost traits: the 911's sensuous shoulders and hips, restored by pulling in the waist and pushing out the track at both axles. The previous 911

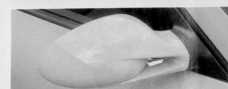

THE VERDICT

Highs: Shaped with some old curves, blatting exhaust, sharper controls, more fun.

Lows: Expensive as always, only 911 nuts may notice you.

The Verdict: More Porsche, less Supra.

looked slightly flaccid, as if one too many strudels had gone to its middle. A 911 has always stirred the blood with svelte, athletic curves stretched tight over large tires. This new Carrera, long-serving Porsche chief designer Harm Lagaay's final opus before retirement, does the stirring a bit better. It has nearly identical length and height dimensions as the outgoing 996 model's, but with its bigger behind, upright oval headlights, and slotted lenses for the front turn signals, it generates similar visual venom to the old air-cooled 993.

The reskin is subtle enough that only other 911 wing nuts will likely notice it at first glance. And the new 997 only *appears* slimmer. At 3290 pounds, this 2005 Carrera S is heavier than its predecessor by about 100 pounds. The standard 19-inch wheels and tires—the last Carrera offered standard 18s—are among the culprits.

In the cockpit Porsche has abandoned its fascination with rising dough forms. The lines are now as hard and straight as the stripes on the German flag, the dash is available with a long, low shelf of French-stitched leather (part of a $4825 leather package that was not on our test

car). Its surfaces are firm and unyielding, the airbags artfully concealed as if time had stopped before the invention of the crash dummy. Thin blades of silver-painted plastic do the accenting around the vent grilles, and two minimalist cup holders, no doubt Nürburgring-tested with a Big Gulp, swing out from behind a narrow door pinched between the dash and glove box. The jet-intake door pulls provide the only real flourish.

Optional steering-wheel controls (for $990) aid the optically challenged and thick-fingered who try to operate the clusters of tiny buttons. At least the quintet of circles that form the gauges fan out in a wider, more handsome spread for easier viewing. A big tach takes the center, of course. The $920 Sport Chrono Package Plus parks a dual analog-digital stopwatch on the dash operated by a steering column lever. Memorize the dense manual in the pits before attempting the lap record. Was that "lever forward" for the lap split, or was it "down and back" to reset? Even with the chronograph's wart there, visibility forward improves, and the cockpit feels more spacious with the overall shrinking and retreating of the dash.

Forward visibility you'll want, since the acceleration of the new Carrera S was more intense than expected. The new 350-hp, 3.8-liter boxer with DOHC variable cam timing and lift employs the same two-piece aluminum block as in the base 321-hp, 3.6-liter Carrera, but with a bore increase of three millimeters, different fuel injectors, and a reshaped air-intake system for smoother flow and lustier sound quality. Torque rises as well, by 22 pound-feet to 295.

Insert the key in its traditional slot to the left of the column. The quad tailpipe tips, distinguishing the Carrera S from the two-pipe Carrera, bark loudly on startup. The whole car shivers lightly at idle, the exhaust clatter raw and raspy. This is the Porsche experience drivers open their wallets for, the ticking and tapping and whirring of expensive parts felt through their Levi's and their fingertips. It had gone dim in the previous 911, as did some tactile satisfaction in the controls.

The previous pistol-handle shifter was a little loose at the roots. The new stick's round knob feels in your palm like a baseball must have felt to Joltin' Joe, and it slips tautly through its gates as if pulled by magnets. In every gear the big six whirls to about 5000 rpm, where it changes to the deep-lift cam and lunges with extra ferocity at the 7200-rpm redline. The last gear stretches to 179 mph.

Even with the rear axle tramping violently almost all the way through first gear, the Carrera S could be horsewhipped to a 4.1-second 60-mph run and a 12.6-second quarter-mile at 112 mph, slightly quicker than the slightly lighter 400-hp C6 Corvette [*C/D*, September 2004]. The old 911 GT3 with 380 horses was but a 10th quicker to 60 and the mighty 415-hp 911 Turbo just 0.2 second. Nominally shorter ratios in the Carrera S's revamped six-speed manual give it extra spurt-ability, but don't try clutch drops with a car you plan to keep.

Do try your favorite Alpine pass in the new 911. The sticky 0.97-g skidpad performance whets the appetite for winding asphalt, and the 911 carves it up smoked. A variable-ratio steering rack speeds up the wheel response at any angle greater than 30 degrees. Weaving down a narrow

street between parked cars, the wheel can feel a little slow. Porsche says this is basically the old 911's ratio: safe, comfortable, no worries about a 70-mph sneeze sending you into the weeds.

Dial in more, and the response rises closer to a hair-trigger rate for fast adjustment midcorner. The transition is transparent, the spacing between the ratios close enough not to notice. Just flow from bend to hairpin to sweeper with as much right foot as you dare. The thin wheel rim still reports with small tugs and twitches, the front tires cutting perfect arcs and the rear end planted firmly on its vast patch of rubber. The flat poise remains under braking, the clamps delivering five successive stops from 70 mph all at less than 160 feet.

The 61.7 percent of the car's weight on the back should want to chart its own loopy course, but Porsche has tamed that tiger so completely that getting the rear end out takes a concentrated attempt at foolishness. It's one that the otherwise

complacent stability control will stop unless you turn it off.

Or set it to sport, which makes the computer even more tolerant of woolly driving, so tolerant that track day may pass without your touching it. The sport mode also firms up the electronically self-adjusting shocks, called Porsche Active Suspension Management. In normal mode, the system is downright supple, varying the valve settings to smooth out

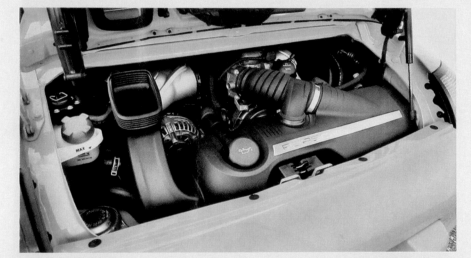

COUNTERPOINT

TONY SWAN

Refinement is a word that gets tossed around pretty freely in the car biz, but I can't think of a better term to sum up the latest 911. The ride quality's hard edges are smoother, the cabin is quieter, the shifting more precise, the look and feel of the interior materials richer. The elements that will score with 911 purists—improved performance and front-end sheetmetal that's not Boxster-esque—are certainly welcome. But for a guy increasingly devoted to hedonism (with no diminution of need for speed), the new 911 scores because it's far more pleasant in day-to-day driving. This is an intensely desirable car. Spare me that paranoia-yellow paint, though.

TONY QUIROGA

The exterior styling of the newest 911 clearly mimics the last of the air-cooled cars. A less obvious but more satisfying change is the new interior. The last-generation 911 had a dash that barely differed from the one in the Boxster. For those Porschephiles, myself included, who had the classic 911 layout burned into their psyche at an early age, the new interior felt alien. Thankfully, Porsche has returned to the spirit of the air-cooled interior in its latest incarnation. I immediately felt as if I'd returned home. The cues are subtle, but it's in the gentle sweep over the five gauges and the lip that runs the length of the dash. To me, it's as welcoming as family.

CSABA CSERE

This 997 version of the Porsche 911 is nothing like the ground-up redesign that the 996 represented six years ago. Yes, this 911 S has a big power bump, more traditional styling, and a richer interior. But the best part of the new model is a greater sense of driver involvement. Drive the 997 over undulating pavement, and its steering works in your hands more than the 996's ever did. Similarly, the 997's shifter feels more tightly coupled to the innards of the gearbox. And when pressed in a corner, the car responds more immediately to subtle adjustments of the throttle. In other words, the 997 is more of a driver's car than the 996 was—and that's saying something.

PORSCHE 911 CARRERA S

Vehicle type: rear-engine, rear-wheel-drive, 2+2-passenger, 2-door coupe

Price as tested: $85,910

Price and option breakdown: base Porsche 911 Carrera S (includes $795 freight), $79,895; Power Seat package, $1550; Bose High End Sound package, $1390; three-spoke multifunctional steering wheel, $990; Sport Chrono Package Plus, $920; heated front seats, $480; auto-dimming mirrors, $385; wheel caps with colored crests, $185; interior-color floor mats, $115

Major standard accessories: power windows, seats, locks, and sunroof; remote locking; A/C; cruise control; tilting and telescoping steering wheel; rear defroster

Sound system: Bose AM-FM radio/CD player, 9 speakers

ENGINE
Type	flat-6, aluminum block and heads
Bore x stroke	3.90 x 3.26 in, 99.0 x 82.8mm
Displacement	233 cu in, 3824cc
Compression ratio	11.8:1
Fuel-delivery system	port injection
Valve gear	chain-driven double overhead cams, 4 valves per cylinder, hydraulic lifters, variable intake-valve timing and lift
Power (SAE net)	350 bhp @ 6600 rpm
Torque (SAE net)	295 lb-ft @ 4600 rpm
Redline	7200 rpm

DRIVETRAIN
Transmission . . . . 6-speed manual
Final-drive ratio . . . . 3.44:1, limited slip

Gear	Ratio	Mph/1000 rpm	Max test speed
I	3.91	5.6	40 mph (7200 rpm)
II	2.32	9.4	68 mph (7200 rpm)
III	1.61	13.6	98 mph (7200 rpm)
IV	1.28	17.1	123 mph (7200 rpm)
V	1.08	20.2	146 mph (7200 rpm)
VI	0.88	24.8	179 mph (7200 rpm)

DIMENSIONS
Wheelbase	92.5 in
Track, front/rear	58.5/59.7 in
Length/width/height	175.6/71.2/51.2 in
Ground clearance	3.8 in
Drag area, Cd (0.29) x frontal area (21.5 sq ft, est)	6.2 sq ft
Curb weight	3290 lb
Weight distribution, F/R	38.3/61.7%
Curb weight per horsepower	9.4 lb
Fuel capacity	16.9 gal

CHASSIS/BODY
Type . . . . . . unit construction with a rubber-isolated subframe
Body material . . . . welded steel stampings

INTERIOR
SAE volume, front seat . . . . . . 48 cu ft
rear seat . . . . . . 16 cu ft
luggage . . . . . . 5 cu ft
Front-seat adjustments . . . . fore-and-aft, seatback angle, front height, rear height, lumbar support
Restraint systems, front . . . . . manual 3-point belts; driver and passenger front, side, and head airbags
rear . . . . manual 3-point belts

SUSPENSION
Front . . . . ind; strut located by a control arm; coil springs; 2-position, cockpit-adjustable shock absorbers; anti-roll bar
Rear . . . . ind; 1 trailing link, 2 lateral links, 1 diagonal link, and 1 toe control link per side; coil springs; 2-position, cockpit-adjustable shock absorbers; anti-roll bar

STEERING
Type . . . . rack-and-pinion with variable ratio and hydraulic power assist
Steering ratio 13.8–17.1:1
Turns lock-to-lock 2.7
Turning circle curb-to-curb . . . . 36.0 ft

BRAKES
Type . . . . hydraulic with vacuum power assist and anti-lock control
Front . . . . . . 13.0 x 1.3-in vented, cross-drilled disc
Rear . . . . . . 13.0 x 1.1-in vented, cross-drilled disc

WHEELS AND TIRES
Wheel size . . . . . . F: 8.0 x 19 in, R: 11.0 x 19 in
Wheel type . . . . . . cast aluminum
Tires . . . . . . Michelin Pilot Sport PS2; F: 235/35ZR-19 87Y N1, R: 295/30ZR-19 100Y N1
Test inflation pressures, F/R . . . . . . 34/40 psi
Spare . . . . . . none

---

ripples. Push the sport button, or just drive faster; the computer reads either signal and turns up the shock resistance. No Porsche before this one has ridden so serenely while also supplying this level of body control.

Can the next 911 possibly provide more, or has the car at last reached its summit, a mix of old and new that is facing a Darwinian dead end? Porsche is selling tradition with the 911. The more the company modernizes and mainstreams it, the less appeal it has for the faithful. Where does the Porsche 911 go from here? Perhaps it doesn't have to go anywhere. ∎

C/D TEST RESULTS

ACCELERATION
	Seconds
Zero to 30 mph	1.5
40 mph	2.0
50 mph	3.1
60 mph	4.1
70 mph	5.1
80 mph	6.0
90 mph	8.2
100 mph	10.2
110 mph	12.2
120 mph	14.4
130 mph	17.7
140 mph	21.1
150 mph	26.4
Street start, 5–60 mph	5.0
Top-gear acceleration, 30–50 mph	7.0
50–70 mph	7.2
Standing ¼-mile	12.6 sec @ 112 mph
Top speed (redline limited)	179 mph

BRAKING
70–0 mph @ impending lockup . . . . 154 ft

HANDLING
Roadholding, 300-ft-dia skidpad . . . . 0.97 g
Understeer . . . . moderate

FUEL ECONOMY
EPA city driving . . . . 18 mpg
EPA highway driving . . . . 26 mpg
C/D-observed . . . . 15 mpg

INTERIOR SOUND LEVEL
Idle . . . . 51 dBA
Full-throttle acceleration . . . . 86 dBA
70-mph cruising . . . . 75 dBA

CURRENT BASE PRICE* dollars x 1000
- Porsche 911 Carrera S
- Jaguar XKR
- Dodge Viper SRT-10
- Maserati Coupé Cambiocorsa

0   20   40   60   80   100
*Base price includes freight, any performance options, and applicable gas-guzzler taxes.

ACCELERATION seconds ■0–60 mph ■ 1/4-mile
- Dodge Viper SRT-10
- Porsche 911 Carrera S
- Maserati Coupé Cambiocorsa
- Jaguar XKR

0   3   6   9   12   15

BRAKING 70–0 mph, feet
- Dodge Viper SRT-10
- Porsche 911 Carrera S
- Maserati Coupé Cambiocorsa
- Jaguar XKR

120   130   140   150   160   170

ROADHOLDING 300-foot skidpad, g
- Dodge Viper SRT-10
- Porsche 911 Carrera S
- Jaguar XKR
- Maserati Coupé Cambiocorsa

0.60   0.70   0.80   0.90   1.00   1.10

EPA CITY FUEL ECONOMY mpg
- Porsche 911 Carrera S
- Jaguar XKR
- Dodge Viper SRT-10
- Maserati Coupé Cambiocorsa

0   4   8   12   16   20

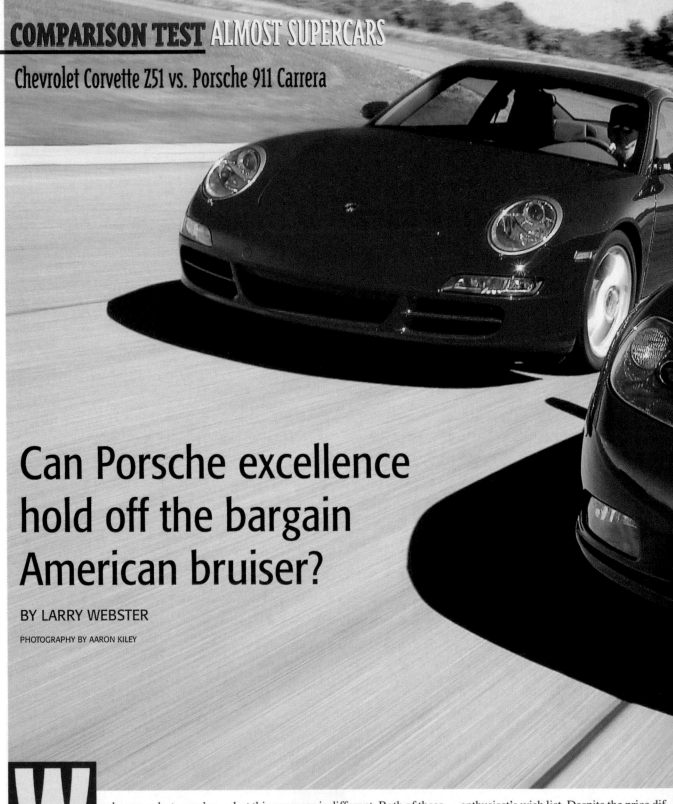

COMPARISON TEST ALMOST SUPERCARS

Chevrolet Corvette Z51 vs. Porsche 911 Carrera

Can Porsche excellence hold off the bargain American bruiser?

BY LARRY WEBSTER

PHOTOGRAPHY BY AARON KILEY

We know what you're thinking: This is not a fair fight. In one corner, there's the American value-packed brute, the $44,245 Corvette. And in the other, a high-priced *über*-coupe, Porsche's latest 911 (code-named 997), which costs a stunning $70,065.

Pitting cars with such wildly unequal prices (the 911 costs *58 percent more* than the Corvette) is not our standard practice,

but this comparo is different. Both of these are fantastically fast sports cars that are almost quick enough to be ranked as supercars but have prices that make them somewhat accessible. And whether they're used for commuting to work in reasonable comfort or getting your g-jollies at the track, these cars can do both jobs. Plus, they're new or, shall we say, extensively updated for 2005. These two legendary models both have an illustrious racing heritage, and they have at some point graced every

enthusiast's wish list. Despite the price difference, they have competed against each other numerous times in these pages (see sidebar).

And to be frank, we needed some real competition to put up against the Vette. Only the $48,995 BMW M3 is even close in performance and price. But the M3's back seat makes it a different kind of car, and even with a sultry 333-hp inline-six, its firepower wouldn't be adequate.

So the task fell to Zuffenhausen's fran-

chise player, the 911. For 2005, a freer-breathing intake system yielded six more ponies from the 3.6-liter aluminum flat-six. The total now stands at 321, with torque the same, at 273 pound-feet. That's 12 fewer horses than the M3 has, but the 911 weighs about 200 fewer pounds.

Thanks to wider fender flares, the 911 has a slightly increased track front and rear. The combination of a front-strut and rear-multilink suspension carries over, but the development process has continued, and

the entire system has been tweaked for the usual claims of a smoother ride and tighter handling.

There's a new interior, there are 18-inch wheels and tires, and finally, Porsche has gone back to the more upright head-light housings that we liked so much in previous models. It's a typical array of detail improvements that Porsche says add up to a major step forward. For the 911's sake, we hope so, because the Vette looks awfully strong.

Although the Vette, too, is an evolu-tionary version, its engine room received a serious bump. The aluminum V-8 is not only larger (5.7 to 6.0 liters) but also has a thumping 400 horses and 400 pound-feet of torque. The previous Vette had 50 fewer horses and 25 fewer pound-feet of torque when coupled to the six-speed manual gearbox.

The Corvette also gets a host of chassis changes, new bodywork, a new interior, and finally, such features as a navigation

Vehicle	Chevrolet Corvette Z51	Porsche 911 Carrera
base price/ price as tested	**$44,245/ $54,240**	$70,065/ $76,195
dimensions, in length	174.6	175.6
width	72.6	71.2
height	49.1	51.6
wheelbase	105.7	92.5
track, front/rear	62.1/60.7	58.5/60.4
weight, pounds	3288	**3253**
weight distribution, % front/rear	52.1/47.9	38.4/61.6
fuel tank, gallons	**18.0**	16.9
recommended octane rating	93	91
interior volume, cu ft front	**52**	48
rear	–	**16**
trunk	**22**	5
Best in test.		

system and heated seats. For a car so capable, the base price of $44,245 is a genuine bargain. Ours came with the $1495 Z51 suspension package that offers shorter transmission ratios, grippier tires, bigger brakes, and a transmission-oil cooler. It's the track hound of the Corvette lineup. In addition, $8500 worth of nonperformance options brought it to a grand total of $54,240.

The 911 arrived with a navigation system, bixenon headlights, a Bose stereo system, and a few other options, for $76,195.

As a couple of advertised do-everything sports cars, we put them through our usual battery of performance tests, along with 500 miles of highway and back-road driving, and since these cars are meant for

the occasional romp at the track and we weren't popping for tires, we spent a day lapping 1.9-mile GingerMan Raceway in South Haven, Michigan.

Don't rush off to the results chart just yet. We made an adjustment to our ballot that needs explaining. It's an attempt to rectify the price discrepancy between these cars.

Our ballot has 21 categories that are worth a varying number of points, from a minimum of five to a maximum of 25. Drivers rate the cars in most categories, and others are calculated from dimensions or test results; then we average the scores and total the points. The car with the highest total wins. In our usual comparison tests, drivers can award a maximum of 10 points in the value category. But as

we noted, the Porsche's base price is 58 percent greater than the Chevrolet's—in a typical comparo the difference is closer to 15 percent. So for this test, the value category has a maximum of 20 points.

Considering that a perfect score in every category would be more than 200 points, this is a small change. But it's one that allowed voters to better consider each car's cost.

So, anyway, enough about points, here's how things played out.

Second Place
Porsche 911 Carrera

The 911's classic, time-weathered shape has never looked better. The wider fenders give a beefy, more purposeful look that complements the silhouette. And the

packaging benefits of the rear-engine layout are as handy as ever. For the first time, the 911 is longer than the Corvette. And the Porsche, at least, still has room for a couple of kids in the back seats.

So when it comes to handling, which is better, an engine in front or in back? For racing, the answer is neither—the mid-engine design is clearly better, as demonstrated by every purpose-built race car. But what about street cars that offer at least some practicality?

We're not going to answer that one because, well, there is no simple answer. Here, both of these cars are fantastic curve carvers. On the street, though, the nod goes to the 911.

We never found a patch of road that gave us even a whiff of that "Oh, %#$@!"

feeling that precedes some type of mid-corner correction or wheel sawing. Editor-at-large Pat Bedard calls this "path accuracy." At speed, how accurately can you place the car? With the 911, the answer is in fractions of an inch; with the Vette, it's in inches. This feeling likely is why the 911 went through the cones of our lane-change test 1.1 mph faster than the Vette. You can plant this car anywhere.

Although we were initially skeptical of the 911's variable-ratio steering, we're believers now. The ratio quickens the farther you turn the wheel, but you don't notice it. The effort is light, but the steering is wonderfully accurate.

Bumps have no effect on trajectory. The suspension is nicely supple and not the least bit floaty. It's a lot like the sus-

2 Porsche 911 Carrera

Highs: Telepathic steering and brake feel, an engine that sounds as good as it performs, you cannot upset this chassis.

Lows: Raising the seat via the manual adjuster tilts it forward, sticker shock.

The Verdict: Deserves to be lusted after.

penders of the BMW 3-series that we like so much. The 911 suspension is stiff enough to keep the chassis movements to a minimum and communicate irregularities to the driver but also resilient enough to absorb bumps and cushion blows. The 911 pulled 0.97 g on the skidpad, a tick less than the Vette's 0.98, but in every subjective handling category except one, the 911 outscored the Vette.

It also trailed the Vette in every speed contest except top-gear acceleration, where the Vette's hugely tall top gear puts the Chevy at a disadvantage. You have to grin and bear the gut-wrenching, axle-hopping launch to make the Porsche go its quickest, but the 911 seems to outperform its spec sheet. The power-to-weight ratio is 23 percent poorer than the Vette's, but the 911's rear weight bias keeps things close until speeds rise. At 60 mph, the

Powertrain			Chevrolet Corvette Z51	Porsche 911 Carrera	
engine		type	pushrod 16-valve V-8	DOHC 24-valve flat-6	
		displacement, cu in (cc)	364 (5967)	219 (3596)	
		power, bhp @ rpm	**400 @ 6000**	321 @ 6800	
		torque, lb-ft @ rpm	**400 @ 4400**	273 @ 4250	
		redline, rpm	6500	7200	
		lb per bhp	**8.2**	10.1	
driveline		transmission	6-sp man	6-sp man	
		driven wheels	rear	rear	
		gear ratios:1	2.97, 2.07, 1.43, 1.00, 0.71, 0.57	3.91, 2.32, 1.61, 1.28, 1.08, 0.88	
		axle ratio:1	3.42	3.44	
		mph/1000 rpm	7.6, 10.9, 15.8, 22.5, 31.8, 39.6	5.7, 9.5, 13.7, 17.3, 20.5, 25.1	
C/D test results	acceleration, seconds	0–60 mph	**4.1**	4.3	4.2
		0–100 mph	**9.6**	10.5	10.1
		0–150 mph	**25.0**	28.5	26.8
		1/4-mile @ mph	**12.6 @ 114**	12.8 @ 109	12.7 @ 11.
		rolling 5–60 mph	**5.1**	5.3	5.2
	top-gear	30–50 mph	10.3	**7.6**	9.0
		50–70 mph	9.6	**7.9**	8.8
		top speed, mph	186 (drag limited, mfr's claim)	181 (redline limited)	184
	sound level, dBA	idle	60	**52**	56
		full-throttle	86	**83**	85
		70-mph cruise	74	76	75
	fuel economy, mpg	EPA city	19	**19**	19
		EPA highway	28	26	27
		C/D 500-mile trip	18	17	18
Best in test.					*Test Avg*

Chassis	Chevrolet Corvette Z51	Porsche 911 Carrera	
front suspension	control arms, leaf spring, anti-roll bar	strut, coil springs, anti-roll bar	
rear suspension	control arms, leaf spring, anti-roll bar	multilink, coil springs, anti-roll bar	
front brakes	vented disc	vented disc	
rear brakes	vented disc	vented disc	
anti-lock control	yes	yes	
stability control	yes	yes	
tires	Goodyear Eagle F1 Supercar EMT; F: P245/40ZR-18 88Y, R: P285/35ZR-19 90Y	Michelin Pilot Sport PS2; F: 235/40ZR-18 91Y, R: 265/40ZR-18 101Y	
C/D test results	braking, 70–0, feet	164	**150**	*157*
	roadholding, 300-foot skidpad, g	**0.98**	0.97	*0.90*
	lane change, mph	66.8	**67.9**	*67.4*
Best in test.			*Test Avg*

Porsche's 4.3-second time is only 0.2 second slower than the Vette's, but at 150, the gap is 3.5 seconds.

The 911, therefore, needed a major handling advantage to outrun the Vette at GingerMan. No such trump card arose. Like most recent 911s, this one predominantly understeers, so in GingerMan's long corners, we had to wait seemingly forever to put the power down and accelerate out of the turns. The 911's best lap time of 1:37.95 was 2.3 seconds slower than the Vette's. That's an eternity in road racing.

Still, we love this Porsche. It has a visceral attitude that's been softened only enough so the car is perfectly livable. We'd need just one hand to count the things we'd change, and the manual seat-height adjuster that tilts the seat as it rises would be *numero dos*.

Numero uno is the price. Would we pay an extra five grand, over the Corvette, for the 911? That's a no-brainer; absolutely. Fifteen? Probably, but we'd have to think about it. Twenty? Well, you already know our answer: no.

First Place
Chevrolet Corvette Z51

We never thought this would be such a close match. After our first test of the C6 Corvette and before we'd piloted the new 911, we figured the Porsche was a mackerel, the Chevy a barracuda. But the Vette won by one measly point.

We even managed to wring a couple of 10ths out of the Vette's already stellar acceleration times. Chevy's sportster knifed to 60 mph in a scant 4.1 seconds, a couple 10ths quicker than the 2005 yellow car we tested in September. This red car was a little slower in top-gear acceleration tests, so we don't think it was a particularly strong example. Or maybe we simply got better at launching it.

It's far from a stoplight special, though. "Very nice highway car—smooth, quiet,

refined. At 80 mph, I can barely hear the engine. Plus, I could easily get comfortable in the new, attractive interior," wrote one tester.

But Chevy hasn't removed all the Vette's traditional character. This is still a brute. For one, you look out over a long,

wide hood. Although the Corvette is an inch shorter than the 911, ask anyone which is longer, and no one will get it right. Between the two, we all preferred the more expansive view out the 911.

You can't argue with the Vette's capabilities, though. On back roads, it can pull

December 1981

AARON KILEY

23 Years of Going Nose to Nose

We have put a 911 against a Corvette five times on these pages. Two of these encounters were multicar comparos, and three were head-to-heads. The first was in December 1981, when we pitted four sports cars against the De Lorean. Even then, the 911's as-tested price of $34,165 seemed audacious when compared with the $19,000 Vette. The horsepower numbers seem puny by today's weaponry standards: 172 for the Porsche and 190 for the Chevy. We didn't pick a winner or rank them, but it was clear the 911 easily had the Vette covered.

Fast-forward to September 1988, and the tide had shifted. Against the 214-hp 911 Club Sport, the 245-hp Corvette Z51 fell behind in acceleration tests but stormed ahead on the race and autocross courses. It was also about 15 grand cheaper, and it won.

Two years later, in a five-car roundup [September 1990], a $59,795, 375-hp ZR-1, dubbed the "Corvette from Hell," finished a hellish third, one spot behind the $80,257, 247-hp 911. Advantage Porsche.

And then a funny thing happened. In April 1991, the ZR-1 went head-to-head with the most powerful 911 of the day, the $105,191, 315-hp turbo model. It should've been a Porsche rout, but it wasn't—the Vette prevailed, due largely to a better-sorted suspension.

The next meeting came in May 1998. The 911 was strong for that meeting, besting the Vette to 60 mph and on the road course. But it wasn't enough to overcome the 30-grand price premium, and the Vette prevailed.

Do Porsche guys care that the score is now four to two for the Vette? Probably not. —LW

May 1998

DAVID DEWHURST

1 Chevrolet Corvette Z51

Highs: Performance that puts most sports cars on the trailer, surprising comfort and value.

Lows: We'd give up some cush for more road feel and a throatier engine note.

The Verdict: Still a great car, but it's not the wunderkind we first thought it was.

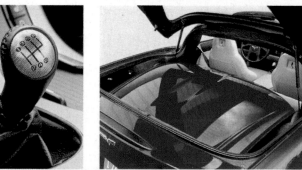

some distance on the 911, but it rea makes you work for it. Two commen from the test-driver logbook: "The 9 doesn't throw you around nearly as mu as the Vette over bumpy curves, and i noticeably more stable." And this: "W the Vette, you have to tell yourself i going to stay glued to the road, but in 911, there's no need to wonder." On smooth racetrack, up-and-down motic were still present and the chassis mov around a lot more than we expected. Pl as in the 911, it was a little tricky to fe in power while coming off the turns, for a different reason. Where the 911 s its front tires, the Corvette was a little t eager to fishtail.

But that was the Vette's only vice, a in some ways it was an advantage. G gerMan has a lot of long, gradual curv and if the Vette started to drift wide of intended arc, a little added power cou rotate the car back on line. We couldn't that in the Porsche. And if we hung out tail a little too far, it took only a quick do of countersteering to put the car straig The brakes, like those on the Porsch didn't exhibit any fade during our five-sessions.

There is, however, a numbness to t chassis that was especially apparent wh

compared with the Porsche, and that cost the Vette some points. The Chevy can be driven extremely quickly, but it doesn't inspire the same confidence as the Porsche. Although both these cars ride quite well, the Vette feels a little less buttoned down. It could use more precision and perhaps stiffer shocks.

The difference was most noticeable while braking. Stomp on the middle pedal in the Vette, and it practically stands on its nose, whereas the Porsche squats hard. The 911 stopped from 70 in only 150 feet, 14 fewer than the Corvette.

True, that difference is due largely to the Porsche's rear-weight bias, but taken as a complete car, the 911 has a tick more sharpness. The Vette's steering is lifeless in comparison to the 911's. Plus, Chevy could have done better with the shifter. The throws are short, but it's stiff, and it balks every once in a while at a gearchange. It's the opposite of the Porsche's precise and easy-moving rod.

We're talking nuances here; the difference in most categories amounted to only a point. The 911's added feel and precision must be what the extra money buys you, because despite the much lower price, the Vette still has more features, such as power seats, adjustable lumbar and side-bolster supports, and a nifty head-up readout showing lateral acceleration.

In the end, though, it was the Vette's outstanding value that carried the day, as it scored 20 points in that category to the 911's 15. It was a deficit the Porsche almost, but not quite, surmounted. As we've said before, for the money, there isn't a better sports car around. ■

Results		Chevrolet Corvette Z51	Porsche 911 Carrera
vehicle	driver comfort (10)	10	9
	front-seat space* (10)	10	8
	ergonomics (10)	9	9
	trunk space* (5)	5	5
	features/amenities* (10)	10	8
	fit and finish (10)	9	10
	styling (10)	9	9
	value (20)	20	15
	total (85)	82	73
powertrain	engine output* (10)	10	8
	performance* (10)	10	8
	throttle response (10)	10	10
	engine NVH (10)	8	10
	transmission (10)	8	10
	total (50)	46	46
chassis	performance* (10)	9	10
	steering feel (10)	8	10
	brake feel (10)	9	10
	on-road handling (10)	9	10
	race-track handling (10)	9	9
	ride (10)	9	10
	total (60)	53	59
	gotta-have-it factor (25)	23	24
	fun to drive (25)	22	23
	grand total (245)	226	225
	finishing order	1	2

*These objective scores are calculated from the vehicles' dimensions, capacities, and/or test results. **Best in test.**

Hey, whaddya get when you combine a Boxster with a 911?

BY PETER ROBINSON

We are requested not to refer to Porsche's latest sports car as a Boxster coupe. Zuffenhausen's marketing gurus insist their new mid-engined two-seater is a stand-alone model, positioned in performance and price between the Boxster S roadster and 911 Carrera coupe. It's so distinctive, they opine, that it deserves a new label. Meet the Cayman S.

In reality, as our photographs demonstrate, it will strike the casual viewer as a coupe version of Porsche's new, second-generation mid-engine ragtop, the Boxster. A tad longer—half an inch—and higher—ditto—and yes, slightly more powerful

(up 15 horsepower), the Cayman shares not only the same basic chassis and front structure with the Boxster but also the lower doors, the front hood and fenders, and the headlights and taillights. No matter, the under-body is much tweaked, suspension settings are tuned to make the most of torsional rigidity that's almost 150 percent stiffer than the already impressive roadster's, and that makes for improved handling and grip without, the engineers claim, any loss in ride comfort.

Potentially, therefore, the Cayman S (named imaginatively for a breed of crocodile, not the remote Caribbean islands) combines the best of the Boxster and 911: the rigidity of a

coupe body (like the Carrera's) combined with the superior weight distribution delivered by the Boxster's mid-engine layout. The brakes and the steering are Boxster S. No arguments here; the S did win a recent sports-car comparo ["It's-All-About-Me Roadsters," *C/D*, March 2005].

To help justify a price significantly higher than that of a Boxster S—some $58,000-plus versus $53,895—Porsche goes back to an earlier variation of the classic flat-six engine that in 3.2- and 3.6-liter forms powers the Boxster and 911. This 3.4-liter engine uses the 96-millimeter bore and 78mm stroke from the first water-cooled 996. Easy. The resulting 291 horsepower at 6200 rpm and 251

pound-feet of torque at 4400 rpm sit neatly between the Boxster S's 276 horsepower and 236 pound-feet and the 3.6-liter Carrera's 321 horsepower and 273 pound-feet.

There's no sign, yet, of Porsche's long-awaited double-clutch manual gearbox (from the same supplier as Audi/VW's DSG) that's now expected to be launched with the latest 911 Turbo later this year. Instead, the final-drive and upper ratios of the six-speed manual are identical to the Boxster's, but first and second ratios are slightly lower. Hans-Jürgen Wöhler, director of the Boxster/Cayman line, says there is no weight increase over the 3080-pound Boxster S. Expect 0-to-60 mph in less than five seconds and

a top speed of 172 mph, again splitting the difference between the Boxster S and 911 Carrera.

Does unveiling the Cayman as a kicked-up S indicate there's a less-powerful version in the pipeline? You bet. Expect a number of Cayman variants, including a 2.7- and/or 3.2-liter entry-level model, plus a lightweight club sport.

All Wolfgang Dürheimer, executive V-P of R&D, says on the subject is, "We don't think with the Cayman we will break with Porsche tradition. The S is the top model for a new product. The strategy of variants works very well on the 911 side. There's no reason it can't be applied to our other model lines."

Subtle styling changes include a

bigger central orifice in front. The divergence between roadster and coupe grows from the windshield rearward. In fact, the windshield is Boxster, except that on the coupe it's set marginally lower, flowing upward into a rounded roofline. A revised side air vent now incorporates a sharp ridge that trails along the doorsill before rising up the vent's trailing edge. The designers have set the angle of the small rear side window to harmoniously complement the vent's steep slope.

The voluptuous rear fenders are marginally higher than the Boxster's and outboard of the coupe's strongly tapered cabin (and the relatively narrow hatchback), creating a gorgeous dip between fender and body. To maximize access to the trunk, the hatch incorporates the rear window, and it's flanked by small outer fins. An almost flat body section runs from the window to a split-wing spoiler that rises like the 911 Turbo's to reduce lift by seven percent over that of the Boxster S. New 18-inch five-spoke alloy wheels are exclusive to the Cayman.

What the Cayman can't have is two-plus-two seating, such as the rear-engined 911's setup. Instead, immediately behind the front buckets

is a carpeted and heavily sound-proofed engine cover, with a chrome safety bar to prevent luggage from sliding forward. The trunk, in fact, is recessed behind the engine. Porsche says there's now room for two golf bags. The dashboard is pure Boxster, with the exception of a perforated hood for the instruments that's raised to further highlight the centrally located tachometer.

Porsche runs against convention in pricing the Cayman coupe roughly $4000 above the Boxster S roadster. Coupe versions of rivals such as the Audi TT, Chrysler Crossfire, and Nissan 350Z are priced about $5000 below their equivalent softtops, and even a 911 cabriolet runs 10 grand more than a 911 coupe. Porsche won't talk numbers, but insiders expect the Cayman (made in Finland by Valmet on the same line that assembles the Boxster) to add about 15,000 annual sales to Porsche's bottom line to potentially top 100,000 worldwide for the first time. We should know if the controversial pricing strategy works within a few months of the Cayman's going on sale in the U.S. in January 2006. By then we'll also know if it's commonly known as the Cayman or as the "Boxster coupe." ∎

Vehicle type: mid-engine, rear-wheel-drive, 2-passenger, 3-door coupe
Estimated base price: $58,000
Engine type: DOHC 24-valve flat-6, aluminum block and heads, port fuel injection
Displacement............207 cu in, 3387cc
Power (SAE net)......291 bhp @ 6200 rpm
Torque (SAE net).....251 lb-ft @ 4400 rpm

Transmissions.......	5-speed automatic with manumatic shifting, 6-speed manual
Wheelbase.....................	95.1 in
Length/width/height......	172.1/70.9/51.5 in
Curb weight..................	3100 lb

Performance ratings (C/D est):
Zero to 60 mph..................4.9 sec
Standing ¼-mile.................13.4 sec
Top speed (drag limited)...........172 mph
Projected fuel economy (C/D est):
EPA city driving..................19 mpg
EPA highway driving...............27 mpg

COMPARISON TEST COUP DE COUPES

Lotus Exige
Porsche Cayman S

Boy toy runs into Porsche pizazz.

BY TONY SWAN

PHOTOGRAPHY BY JEFFREY G. RUSSELL

Wait a minute, who called this meeting? Porsche Cayman S versus Lotus Exige? Track toy versus this new Porsche that's not quite a 911 but pretty damn close? You guys can*not* be serious.

It's true that the commonalities here aren't quite as comprehensive as you normally see—and we normally prefer—in most of our comparos. But the major comparative points are here: two seats, mid-engine, sports-car heritage, sports-car capabilities, and similar pricing. And if you think *contrasto* instead of *comparo,* it's easier to digest.

It was certainly easy enough to digest as an assignment. Oh—leave the frozen tun-

dra of Michigan in mid-December for the benign climate of Georgia? Three days of putting a couple of brand-new sports cars through their paces? Including a day at Road Atlanta? Well, okay, guess we'll just have to leave that snow-blower repair for later.

Fact is, we had the same sense of mismatch going in as you may have right now. Like other Porsches, the Cayman hasn't forgotten its racing roots. But it hasn't forgotten that at least some owners might consider it as their one and only automobile, either. Which means the designers had to pay attention to mundane nonracing considerations such as NVH, luggage space, and even ride quality. In the every-

day motoring world, man does not live by maximum lateral g alone.

The Lotus Exige pretty much ignores all the foregoing. It pays only the sketchiest lip service to the notion of achieving desirable ride quality, and luggage space is a joke, and who the hell cares about NVH when we're having all this *fun?* Hey, it's s'pozta make noise. You ever hear of a race car that didn't make noise? Where you from, dude?

We confess that we more or less misunderstood the Lotus concept when we first beheld the Exige at the Geneva auto show in 2004. Ah, an Elise with a fixed roof. More civilization, right? A little more viable as an all-around car, right?

Wrong. The top on the Exige is more

permanently in place than the one that covers occupants in the Elise, in the sense that it's hard and bolted into place. Still, if it's a sunny day and you care to take the time to unbolt it, it's removable. Just leave it in the garage, and pray the sun keeps shining. And don't stray too far from home.

More important, the Exige makes no more concession to wussy creature comfort than the Elise. You're paying the extra $8000 for stuff that has nothing to do with comfort, unless we're talking about rarefied situations, such as feeling comfortable negotiating the downhill onto the Road Atlanta front straight close to flat out.

More on that later. But first, the weather report. We referred to Georgia's peachy meteorologics, and we actually experienced some of same on our arrival day, cruising to Atlanta Dragway in bright sunshine and about 60 degrees ambient. *Perfecto.*

It wasn't quite as wonderful the next day at Road Atlanta, as temperatures hovered in the mid-30s and clouds obscured the sun. Not a salubrious prescription for photography, but it didn't hold us back from lapping Road Atlanta's 2.54-mile layout, certainly one of the most entertaining and challenging circuits in this or any other country.

Day three, however, was fuhgedaboudit. The weather gurus were predicting rain, snow, and sleet overnight, and events vindicated the forecast. Driving a Lotus Exige with sticky low-profile Yokohama performance tires on icy roads or in standing water is about as much fun as walking a high wire treated with WD-40. We packed up and headed for the airport.

But even though the public-road component of this, uh, *confronto* was abbreviated, we emerged with a solid consensus regarding the results.

Second Place
Lotus Exige

You don't even have to see this car to understand its character; just check the features list—or, more accurately, what's absent from that list. No power steering. No power-seat adjustment. No power mirrors. No cruise control. No auto-dim inside mirror. No glove box. No map pockets. No automatic climate control. No cup holders, at least not as standard equipment.

Minimalism in a $52,000 car? What's up with that? No mystery, really. You don't see power mirrors, cruise control, cup holders, and such in race cars, and that's the essence of the Exige. It meets minimal standards for street use, but its main task is to deliver optimal performance on a race-track or autocross course. That also applies to the Lotus Elise. So what do you get for the extra $8000?

In a sense, you get vaporware. Although the Exige and the Elise employ the same rigid frame and interior layout, they share almost no body panels. The only commonalities are the outer door skins and the rocker panels. Beyond that, every inch

of the Exige's polymeric epidermis was sculpted to increase downward aero pressure, which builds in direct ratio to speed. The faster you go, the more the air presses the car onto the pavement, which magnifies its grip.

The main elements in the Exige's aero advantage are the front splitter and the big rear wing, and the payoff can be expressed on paper. According to Lotus wind-tunnel data, at 100 mph the Elise has 8.6 pounds of aero downforce at the front, 4.4 pounds at the rear. When the Exige is going the same speed, there are 42.5 pounds squashing down the front end and 48.2 pounds on the rear.

But those are just numbers. The practical effect is far more persuasive, particularly in fast corners. Where the Elise is balanced on a pinpoint, the Exige hunkers down and sticks to the track like quick-dry paint.

This does wonders for a driver's confidence, and it also makes for some surprising on-track results. Road Atlanta is a horsepower track, and we expected the Cayman's big edge in horsepower to translate into quicker lap times. And it did, although not by as much as we had anticipated. The difference was just 2.7 seconds,

Vehicle		Lotus Exige	Porsche Cayman S
	base price/ price as tested	**$51,860/ $55,955**	$59,695/ $70,505
dimensions, in	length	149.5	172.1
	width	68.1	70.9
	height	45.6	51.4
	wheelbase	90.5	95.1
	track, front/rear	57.3/59.3	58.5/60.2
	weight, pounds	**1946**	2974
	weight distribution, % front/rear	37.4/62.6	44.1/55.9
	fuel tank, gallons	10.6	**19.6**
	recommended octane rating	91	91
interior volume, cu ft	front	41	**48**
	luggage	4	**14**
Best in test.			

most of it bound up in the Cayman's superior speed down the long (0.8 mile) back straight. But the Exige was quicker in the twisty sections (see track map, page 78) and handled directional changes as deftly as a ferret chasing a rat through a maze.

Inevitably, the price for aerodynamic downforce is aerodynamic drag, which plays a negative role in straightaway speed. When the Cayman hit the braking zone for turn 10A, we saw indicated speeds of 135 and 136 mph. At the same point the Exige's speedo never went above 124. Lotus lists a governor-limited top speed of 147 mph for the Exige. We think you'd need a Bonneville Salt Flats straightaway to see this.

Which brings us to an allied issue. We were disappointed with the Exige's acceleration times, which were much slower than the Elise we tested in July 2004 ("Extreme

Sports"). We measured a 0-to-60-mph time of 5.2 seconds compared with 4.4, even though this 1946-pound Exige weighed in just 16 pounds heavier than that Elise. Part of this disparity we put down to tricky launch conditions at Atlanta Dragway. But the bigger issue, a soft point with both the Elise and Exige, is the 1.8-liter Toyota engine bolted behind the cockpit.

Lotus has done a lot of work with the ECU to enhance power and durability, but there's still an on/off feel to what happens when the aggressive cam lobes go to work (about 6500 rpm), and there's still not much going on below that threshold.

One logbook comment summed up our collective response. "Terrific chassis,

but every time I drive one of these, I wish Lotus had used a Honda powertrain."

Some elements of the Exige's on-track superiority translate to virtues on the street. Quick, precise steering, for example, is welcome anytime, anywhere. The Exige's wide-open forward sightlines are exemplary, and the updated pedal layout yields better spacing and is also heel-and-toe perfect.

But other elements get old in a hurry. Vision out the back window, which is covered by a mesh screen and further obscured by the wing, induces paranoia. Interior noise levels range from loud to raucous. The absence of seatback and steering-wheel adjustability limits comfort,

Lotus Exige

Highs: Race-car responses, race-car brakes, race-car grip, race-car soul.

Lows: Race-car creature comforts, race-car noise, limited rear view.

The Verdict: A one-dimensional sports car that's almost irresistible in its one dimension.

Powertrain			Lotus Exige	Porsche Cayman S	
engine		type	DOHC 16-valve inline-4	DOHC 24-valve flat-6	
		displacement, cu in (cc)	110 (1796)	207 (3387)	
		power, bhp @ rpm	190 @ 7800	**291** @ 6250	
		torque, lb-ft @ rpm	138 @ 6800	**251** @ 4400	
		redline, rpm	8500	7200	
		lb per bhp	**10.2**	**10.2**	
driveline		transmission	6-sp man	6-sp man	
		driven wheels	rear	rear	
		gear ratios:1	3.12, 2.05, 1.48, 1.17, 0.92, 0.82	3.31, 1.95, 1.41, 1.13, 0.97, 0.82	
		axle ratio:1	4.53	3.88	
		mph per 1000 rpm	5.0, 7.5, 10.5, 13.2, 16.8, 18.9	5.8, 9.9, 13.6, 17.0, 19.8, 23.5	
C/D test results	acceleration, seconds	0–60 mph	**5.2**	5.3	5.3
		0–100 mph	14.2	**12.2**	13.2
		0–110 mph	17.9	**15.1**	16.5
		¼-mile @ mph	13.9 @ 99	**13.6** @ 105	13.8 @ 102
		rolling 5–60 mph	6.1	**5.7**	5.9
	top-gear	30–50 mph	8.1	**8.1**	8.1
		50–70 mph	8.5	**6.7**	7.6
		top speed, mph	147 (gov ltd, mfr's claim)	**171** (drag ltd, mfr's claim)	159
	sound level, dBA	idle	59	**52**	56
		full-throttle	92	**83**	88
		70-mph cruise	78	**72**	75
	fuel economy, mpg	EPA city	24	20	22
		EPA highway	29	28	29
		C/D 250-mile trip	13	10	12
Best in test.					test avg

1 Porsche Cayman S

Highs: All-around drivability, Porsche power, Porsche sounds.

Lows: Nervous at the limit, presumptuous pricing.

The Verdict: Think Porsche 911 with better engine placement for less money.

ride quality is close to race-car stiff, and luggage space is sufficient to accommodate your helmet and driver-suit bag, *period.* If you need anything else, well, that's why we have credit cards.

Perhaps this sounds harsh. Maybe, but Lotus makes no attempt to pretend the Exige is anything but an instrument for enhancing your act at the track. And within that narrow context, the Exige is a champ.

First Place
Porsche Cayman S

The Cayman, for its part, is the champ everywhere else.

We've been anticipating this car's U.S. arrival for more than a year at this writing, including a preview road test in Europe late last year (November 2005). So let's just summarize the pedigree. This is Porsche's hardtop version of the Boxster S. It's stiffer, thanks to a steel cross beam at midships and a hard roof. It's also more

powerful: 291 horsepower and 251 pound-feet of torque, compared with 276 and 236, thanks to an extra 208cc in the Cayman's DOHC 24-valve flat-six engine (3387 versus 3179).

It's also lighter than the Boxster S. Porsche says by 10 pounds. But the last Boxster S we tested ("It's-All-About-Me Roadsters," March 2005) weighed in at 3080 pounds. This Cayman S weighed just 2974.

You'd expect all this to add up to a distinct edge in acceleration for the Cayman, but not so. Our test car needed 5.3 seconds to reach 60 mph, a couple 10ths slower than the Boxster S, and its quarter-mile performance was only marginally better: 13.6 seconds, the same as the Boxster, but a couple mph faster at the lights, 105 versus 103. However, as with the Exige, we suspect Atlanta Dragway launch conditions held the car back a smidge. Last fall's

Cayman test numbers were a wink better.

But those distinctions are academic. As drag-strip speed soared, the Cayman predictably prevailed over the Exige. And no one could possibly call the Cayman slow. As we noted in our November preview, the Cayman S isn't as quick as a basic 911 Carrera, which has 30 more horses. Call us crazy, but we suspect this speed disparity was deliberate on Porsche's part. Nevertheless, 291 horsepower gets the Cayman out of the blocks with gratifying urgency, and the engine emits that deliciously urgent whiskey tenor note that's almost as important as the car's performance. Almost.

At Road Atlanta, the Cayman performed about as expected. The intervention threshold of the stability-control system is commendably high—we used it for a few warm-up laps—but with the assist systems off, and the sport mode switched on, the Cayman was, predictably, quicker.

ROAD ATLANTA

2.54-mile road course, 12 turns

Through Turns One, Two, and Three the cars post identical times. The Exige has sightly higher cornering speeds, but the Cayman makes up time during acceleration.

Both cars reach 100 mph through the Esses and exit Turn Five at 63 mph. But the Cayman shows its brawn once again on the straight uphill section leading to Turn Six, and the Exige loses 0.5 second.

Turn Seven leads to the long, back straightaway, and a high exit speed is essential. The Exige is going 44 mph versus 41 mph for the Cayman.

The Exige falls 1.7 seconds behind on the back straight. Max speeds:
Cayman 138 mph
Exige 121 mph

The Exige carries more speed through the tight 10a and 10b corners, but the Porsche catches up and gets through the uphill section following 10b 0.1 second quicker. Both cars go through Turn 12 at about 95 mph.

On the front straight, the Lotus loses 0.4 second as the Porsche pulls away. The Cayman attains 119 mph, and the Exige reaches 112 mph.

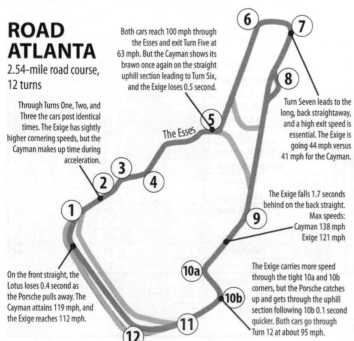

Chassis		Lotus Exige	Porsche Cayman S	
	front suspension	control arms, coil springs, anti-roll bar	strut, coil springs, anti-roll bar	
	rear suspension	control arms, coil springs, anti-roll bar	strut, coil springs, anti-roll bar	
	front brakes	vented, cross-drilled disc	vented, cross-drilled disc	
	rear brakes	vented, cross-drilled disc	vented, cross-drilled disc	
	anti-lock control	yes	yes	
	stability control	no	yes	
	tires	Yokohama Advan A048; F: 195/50R-16 84W, R: 225/45R-17 90W	Michelin Pilot Sport PS2; F: 235/35ZR-19 (87Y), R: 265/35ZR-19 (94Y)	
C/D test results	braking, 70–0, feet	168	**165**	167
	2.5-mile road course, lap time/mph	1:46.7/85.7	**1:44.0/87.9**	1:45.4/86.8
	roadholding, 300-foot skidpad, g	**1.03**	0.96	1.00
	lane change, mph	**65.4**	63.9	64.7
Best in test.				test avg

Not so predictably, it was also scarier. In his preview test, our man Robinson reported driving the Cayman at the Nürburgring's unforgiving Nordschleife, where he observed that it was *"glued"* to the pavement. Our Georgia Cayman had good grip—its 19-inch Michelin PS2s pulled 0.96 g on the skidpad—but on Road Atlanta's Turn 12, the fast downhill righthander onto the front straight, it was far from glued. Hanging on by its toenails is more like it. In contrast to the Exige, trying to keep the Cayman's throttle open in that turn was an exercise in peril. Where the Exige felt stable, the Porsche was comparatively loose. Where the Exige communicated its responses and capabilities with absolute clarity, the Cayman's dynamics were relatively muffled. All in all, it was a textbook illustration of the difference between a single-purpose car and one that must function in multiple environments.

On public roads, of course, the Exige was simply not in the game. Although the Cayman is unquestionably a sports car, and a Porsche sports car at that, it's supple compared with the Lotus. The steering lacks the sense of connection that goes with the Exige's unassisted rack-and-pinion system, but it's far from numb. Beyond that, the Cayman has all the features you'd expect in what is, after all, a luxury sports

car: power adjustments, superb leather-clad seats, an audio system you can actually hear (it's superfluous in the Exige), easy ingress and egress (the Exige requires contortions), and even luggage space, 14 cubic feet split between the front and rear.

It's also a very good-looking Porsche. From the A-pillar forward, it's a family look, but the rear roofline and those powerful haunches are unique to the Cayman, and the going-away view is arguably the sexiest perspective in the current Porsche lineup.

With a base price of $59,695, the Cayman S starts $4200 north of the Boxster S. You don't have to check many boxes on a Porsche order sheet to produce big price escalations, and that was true of our test car, which arrived with a resounding $70,505 tag. We continue to wonder why Porsche prices the coupe so much higher than the softtop Boxster, since the latter is undoubtedly more expensive to produce. Our theory is they do it because they can.

On the other hand, having spent more time with this seductively complete Porsche, we wonder how many first-time Porsche coupe prospects will want to pony up the additional $12,400 required for a base 911 Carrera. If this describes you, save your money. We can practically guarantee that the Cayman S will make you happy. ∎

Results		Lotus Exige	Porsche Cayman S
vehicle	driver comfort (10)	8	10
	ergonomics (10)	9	9
	trunk* (5)	1	5
	features/amenities* (10)	6	10
	fit and finish (10)	7	10
	interior styling (10)	8	10
	exterior styling (10)	10	10
	rebates/discounts* (5)	0	0
	as-tested price* (20)	20	15
	total (90)	69	79
powertrain	¼-mi acceleration* (20)	19	20
	flexibility* (5)	4	5
	fuel economy* (5)	5	4
	engine NVH (10)	6	10
	transmission (10)	8	8
	total (50)	42	47
chassis	performance* (20)	20	18
	steering feel (5)	5	4
	brake feel (5)	5	4
	handling (10)	10	8
	ride (10)	7	10
	total (50)	47	44
	gotta-have-it factor (25)	22	24
	fun to drive (25)	25	22
	grand total (240)	205	216
	finishing order	2	1

*These objective scores are calculated from the vehicles' dimensions, capabilities, rebates and discounts, and/or test results. **Best in test.**

10best 10BEST

CAR AND DRIVER

ONCE AGAIN, WE CATALOG THE BEST ANTIDOTES FOR THE AUTOMOTIVE BLAHS.

BY TONY SWAN
PHOTOGRAPHY BY AARON KILEY

CARS

81

PORSCHE
BOXSTER AND CAYMAN

SPORTS-CAR PURITY.

» The hallmark of a true sports car is how well it involves its driver in the driving. Although the Boxster and the Cayman differ in character—roadster versus hardtop—they're alike in terms of how well they communicate every nuance of mechanical information to the pilots and how accurately they convert driver inputs into response. This is the essence of the car-and-driver connection, and few sports cars do it better.

Neither of these mechanically identical mid-engined cousins can be called inexpensive. Pricing for a basic Boxster,

with a 245-hp, 2.7-liter flat-six, isn't much under $50,000, and a loaded Cayman S easily surpasses $70,000. But we have yet to meet an owner who thinks his car isn't worth the money.

This is the 10th 10Best appearance for the Boxster, and the third straight for the Cayman. Aside from several electronic comfort/convenience options—XM satellite radio and Bluetooth, iPod, MP3, and USB connectivity—both cars enter the 2009 model year unchanged. However, direct injection and dual-clutch automated manual gearboxes are expected to be on the list of mechanical particulars sometime in early '09.

VEHICLE TYPE: mid-engine, rear-wheel-drive, 2-passenger, 2-door roadster or 3-door hatchback

ESTIMATED BASE PRICE: $47,000–$61,000

ENGINES: DOHC 24-valve 2.7-liter flat-6, 245 hp, 201 lb-ft; DOHC 3.4-liter flat-6, 295 hp, 251 lb-ft

TRANSMISSIONS: 5-speed auto with manumatic shifting, 5- or 6-speed manual

DIMENSIONS:
Wheelbase: 95.1 in Length: 171.6–172.1 in
Width: 70.9 in Height: 50.9–51.4 in
Curb weight: 2900–3100 lb

FUEL ECONOMY:
EPA city/highway driving . . . . . 18–20/25–29 mpg

» I DIDN'T EXPECT THAT

PONTIAC G8 GT

It's an old story that dates back nearly 100 years: V-8 meets ordinary car and transforms it into an overnight success. I probably should not have been so surprised by a 361-hp rear-drive sedan that is cut from the same cloth that BMW used to use. But up until 10Best week, my G8 experience had been limited to the mild-mannered V-6 model, which, for all its merits, won't leave you grinning stupidly like the GT will. Think of it this way: The V-8 takes the G8 from being darn good to damn good. —*Tony Quiroga*

cayenne.com/turbo

Sacrifices weight, and that's it for sacrifices.

Every single ounce of the new 500 hp Cayenne Turbo serves one purpose: pure driving performance. Its sports car lines, powerful stance and completely redesigned interior leave no room for excess. And the new Cayenne Turbo is over 400 lbs lighter and more agile than ever. Yet all this performance comes with an impressive new level of efficiency, including a new fuel-saving Auto Start Stop function. Porsche Intelligent Performance means you won't have to surrender a single thing to sports car passion. Porsche. There is no substitute.

The new Porsche Cayenne Turbo

PORSCHE
INTELLIGENT
PERFORMANCE

PORSCHE

2010 PORSCHE PANAMERA

HOT HERETIC

A 911 FOR THE S-CLASS CROWD.

BY JUERGEN ZOELLTER
PHOTOGRAPHY BY CHRISTOPH BAUER

t's finally here, and the big question is this: Is the Panamera a sports car or a fancy four-door?

"This car has the genes of the 911," offers Michael Steiner, the product line director for the Panamera, Porsche's first-ever four-door. Technically a five-door hatchback, this so-called sedan is closely related to the Cayenne SUV, but the Turbo we're driving through a set of switchbacks over the mountains near Cape Town in South Africa does a passable impression of a 911. We're with Steiner and his team as they carry out a 2800-mile final evaluation drive with a Panamera 4S and a

Turbo, both of which have all-wheel drive.

The company's first attempt at a sedan in its 61-year history, the Panamera will come to the U.S. in two forms: the S model, powered by a 400-hp, 4.8-liter naturally aspirated V-8, with either rear- or all-wheel drive (4S), and an all-wheel-drive, twin-turbocharged V-8 version making 500 horses. Both models come with the PDK dual-clutch seven-speed transmission that was recently introduced in the 911. The S model has a six-speed-manual option in Europe that won't be available here initially. The S will start at $89,800, the 4S at $93,800, and a Turbo will set you back $132,600 (not including to-be-determined destination charges).

A 300-hp, 3.6-liter V-6 model will be available at a later date, as will a hybrid that combines Audi's supercharged 333-hp, 3.0-liter V-6 with a 52-hp electric motor for a maximum output of 374 horsepower.

Slipping into a Panamera is more like entering a 911 than a luxury sedan. The front seats are just 1.2 inches higher than in the 911 but lower than those of its competitors (BMW 7-series, Lexus LS460, Maserati Quattroporte, Mercedes S-class). The 911 look is clearly carried over in the instrument panel, with its array of five round dials; the center stack is also recognizable. The transmission tunnel, however, has a battery of switches and buttons that are more logical and less gimmicky than the rotary dials found in the

BMW 7-series and Mercedes S-class.

A shock is the roominess of the back-seat area. Porsche boss Wendelin Wiedeking, a tall and substantial man, had barked about cramped headroom, so design chief Michael Mauer raised the roofline by 0.8 inch. Small as that sounds, it likely accounts for the awkward look to the Panamera's rear quarters. It's a wide car, at 76.0 inches, which adds to this feeling of spaciousness. Cargo room, too, is good: 16 cubic feet in the S model, 15 in the Turbo. With the rear seats folded, all Panameras have 45 cubic feet of luggage space.

So, does the Panamera meet the challenge of driving like a true Porsche? Steiner says the company tried to keep down the weight, using aluminum for the hood, doors, and some suspen-

sion pieces, as well as employing some magnesium castings. Porsche claims the S weighs in just north of 3900 pounds, the Turbo at 4350.

That's a lot lighter than the 4910 pounds of the last Mercedes S63 AMG we tested—however, the Benz is more than nine inches longer—so it's no surprise that Porsche is claiming some impressive performance numbers. The regular S will reportedly rip to 60 mph in 5.2 seconds on its way to a top speed of 175 mph. The 4S shaves 0.4 second off that sprint, its top speed unchanged. The Turbo claim is for a top speed of 188 mph and a 0-to-60 time of 4.0 seconds—a substantial half-second faster

than we managed in the S63 AMG.

Fast as it is, the Panamera is almost hushed as it goes about its business. But never fear: For customers who like thrilling sound effects to go with straight-line fury, Porsche has a way. There's an exhaust button on the center console that activates a valve on each muffler, opening a bypass that produces a much more Porsche-like roar. In the audio department, the Turbo mostly generates a low-frequency buzz as it cruises along between 1200 and 2000 rpm. To get any aural feedback from the Turbo, you have to get into the throttle in a big way. The naturally aspirated engine sounds a lot more satisfying.

It's no surprise that the Panamera is equipped with a complete collection of Porsche driving aids, including stability control (Porsche Stability Management, or PSM), an adjustable damping system (Porsche Active Suspension Management, or PASM), and an adaptive air suspension with an active anti-roll stability system (Porsche Dynamic Chassis Control, or PDCC), which is shared with the Cayenne sport-ute.

With the PASM system in normal mode, the Panamera rides comfortably, although it's firmer than an S-class Benz yet softer than a Maserati Quattroporte Sport GT S. Switching into sport mode, this Porsche's chassis adds feedback—aided by nicely weighted steering that's evocative of a 911's—without ruining the ride.

Hard-core owners, however, will keep their Panamera Turbos in sport plus. For one, it's the only mode in which the Turbo steps off in first gear instead of second. This mode also holds the engine higher up in the rev range before gears are shifted in automatic mode, while in sport and normal modes, light-throttle upshifts happen before the tach needle hits 2000 rpm.

This sport plus mode clearly positions the Panamera to provide a genuine 911 experience without behaving as nervously as the short-wheelbase coupe. With a claimed 52/48 percent front-to-rear weight distribution, the handling balance is nicely neutral, and the car drives much smaller than its size suggests. Porsche's Steiner says that if a driver switches off the stability-control system, the car will oversteer in a controllable manner. Ceramic-composite brake discs will be available with 19- or 20-inch wheels and tires—the base S rides on 245/50ZR-18 front and 275/45ZR-18 rear tires—but the standard brake setup, borrowed from the 911 Turbo, is powerful and responsive.

Just like serious sports cars, the Panamera is equipped with a launch-control system. All models, including U.S.-spec cars, also come with a start/stop system, which uses a conventional but higher-capacity starter motor. As soon as the Panamera comes to a stop, the system shuts off the engine, then restarts very softly when the driver lifts his foot off the brake. It's an industry first for a V-8 engine connected to a transmission other than a manual, as well as a first for the U.S. market.

For high-speed stability, the Panamera Turbo is equipped with an active spoiler, called the "3-D spoiler." It pops up above 50 mph and remains in the so-called "eco position" up to 112 mph. Above that speed, the spoiler extends widthwise to reduce lift, "creating 61 pounds of downforce at 155 mph," according to Steiner.

The 195.7-inch-long Panamera is a unique entry in the luxury-sedan market. It isn't rough and ready like the beautiful Quattroporte, nor is it a techno-geek's dream like the 7-series. And neither does it feel as vaultlike as an S-class Mercedes. But it may have enough 911 DNA to satisfy Porsche enthusiasts and people looking for something different in this market. ●

VEHICLE TYPE: front-engine, rear- or 4-wheel-drive, 4-passenger, 5-door hatchback

ESTIMATED BASE PRICE: $90,600–$133,400

ENGINES: DOHC 32-valve 4.8-liter V-8, 400 hp, 369 lb-ft; twin-turbocharged and intercooled DOHC 32-valve 4.8-liter V-8, 500 hp, 516 lb-ft

TRANSMISSION: 7-speed dual-clutch automated manual

DIMENSIONS:
Wheelbase: 115.0 in Length: 195.7 in
Width: 76.0 in Height: 55.8 in
Curb weight: 3950–4350 lb

PERFORMANCE (MFR'S EST):
Zero to 60 mph . . . . 4.0–5.2 sec
Top speed (drag limited) . . . . . . 175–188 mph

PROJECTED FUEL ECONOMY (C/D EST):
EPA city driving . . . . 13–16 mpg
EPA highway driving . . . . 19–23 mpg

**From behind the wheel,
the resemblance is uncanny.**

It's everything we've learned in six decades of racing transferred to the
street. A lowered suspension and broader stance matched to 405 hp and
21-inch wheels. The new Cayenne GTS. For further evidence of its performance
DNA, visit porscheusa.com/bloodlines. Porsche. There is no substitute.

The new Cayenne GTS

PORSCHE

PREVIEW

WHALE DONE

AFTER 35 YEARS AND SIX GENERATIONS OF TURBOS, PORSCHE STILL FINDS MUCH TO IMPROVE. DON'T LET THE MILDLY REVISED LOOKS FOOL YOU.

40

Porsche introduced the 911 Turbo 35 years ago in Europe, shortly after the first fuel crisis and in the thick of a worldwide crackdown on automotive smog emissions. The company expected to sell only 500 examples of that first Turbo, which was launched with a then-generous 247 SAE horsepower.

Now, six generations and 80,000 Turbos later, Porsche is upgrading the car once again. Though it's a midcycle update rather than a full model change, the improvements are substantial and consequential.

As always, the engine is the star, and for the first time it shares the same construction as the standard 911 engines, which were themselves updated last year. This means the cylinder blocks are now integrated with the crankcase halves, the elaborate dry-sump lubrication system has been replaced by a simpler version used on standard 911s, and the Nikasil cylinder-wall coating is supplanted by the etched hard surface of the Alusil casting system.

The benefits are fewer parts and reduced weight. Furthermore, the engine's displacement increases from 3600 to 3800cc due to bore and stroke dimensions that are identical to those of the current Carrera S.

The engine also gets direct fuel injection, which is particularly beneficial in a turbocharged engine because the cooling effect of the fuel vaporizing in the cylinder allows for an increased compression ratio—up from 9.0:1 to 9.8:1. An intake manifold adapted from the GT2 uses expansion chambers in the intake runners to further cool the incoming charge. Larger intake valves, revised turbochargers, more efficient intercoolers, and a refined exhaust system further improve throughput.

The new engine is about 26 pounds lighter than the previous one, quite an achievement with the direct-fuel-injection system adding 18 pounds—blame the heavier components required by its 2000-psi operating pressure. Peak power rises from 480 to 500 horsepower, and torque is up from

by **ROBERT RICH**
photography by **MARK BRAMLEY**

41

460 to 479 pound-feet despite a drop in maximum boost pressure from 14.5 to 11.6 psi. With the Sport Chrono package, an overboost function raises peak torque to 516 pound-feet for up to 10 seconds. EPA fuel-economy tests haven't yet been completed, but consumption on the European tests has been reduced by 11 percent with the six-speed manual gearbox.

The new model also gets a beefed-up version of Porsche's PDK seven-speed, dual-clutch automated manual. Compared with the unit in the 911s, it has clutch plates that are larger in diameter, with an extra pair in each pack, along with taller ratios in third through sixth gears to better match the Turbo's elevated output. With this gearbox, European fuel-economy figures have improved by 16 percent compared with those of the old car, which used a traditional five-speed automatic transmission, now retired.

An optional, new three-spoke PDK sport steering wheel ($490) with large, separate shift paddles is the way to go and addresses complaints about the somewhat cumbersome shift buttons on the wheel in use with the PDK transmission in the Carrera models.

A revised suspension and a new feature to enhance handling fix some of the dynamic issues we've complained about on the previous car. The software that controls the BorgWarner all-wheel-drive system now allows more rear-tire slip before it sends torque forward, thereby reducing interference with a competent driver's steering corrections. The sus-

INSIDE THE NEW FLAT-SIX

SMOOTHER AND COOLER
More efficient intercoolers have reduced flow restriction while achieving greater temperature reduction.

DIRECT INJECTION
Injectors spray fuel directly into the cylinders across the top of the piston crowns at 2000 psi.

INTEGRAL CYLINDERS
For the first time, the turbo engine employs cylinders that are integral to the crankcase rather than those with separate castings.

LIGHTER VALVETRAIN
Though the intake valves increase from 37.0 to 39.5mm for better flow, smaller-diameter tappets cut valvetrain weight enough to raise the redline from 6600 to 7000 rpm.

SEVEN OIL PUMPS
This 911 Turbo trades its remote-reservoir dry-sump oiling system for a version of the system introduced on the 911 last year. Two scavenge pumps for each cylinder head and one for each turbocharger sump (right) return oil to an isolated reservoir at the bottom of the crankcase. An electronically regulated pressure pump provides the engine's lubrication.

The 911 Turbo now offers distinctive center-lug wheels, as on the 911 GT3. The new, optional PDK sport steering wheel comes with proper paddle shifters.

pension also gets stiffer front anti-roll bars, a softer rear bar, stiffer and variable-rate rear springs, and recalibrated adjustable shocks. The changes are designed to reduce rear-suspension movement during hard driving and improve stability without compromising ride quality.

The aforementioned new feature, called Porsche Torque Vectoring, can gently apply the brake on the inside rear wheel to minimize understeer while entering corners if it seems necessary after monitoring steering angle, vehicle speed, throttle position, and yaw rate. It phases out above 75 mph and is inactive by 100 mph. It's a $1320 option.

These features are all hidden beneath the skin of the Turbo, which is largely unchanged from the previous version. Daytime running lights using LEDs now reside where the previous fog lights did. The headlights can swivel to track the car's path on a winding road. The mirrors are new, as are the taillights, which also use LEDs. And larger exhausts complement the more powerful engine.

The most obvious way to make a 2010 Turbo stand out is to specify the new optional wheels—the 19-inch RS Spyder design ($3835). They have an open-spoke pattern to better reveal the big Porsche brakes and also feature center-lock mounting.

If the visual differences are subtle, the dynamic changes are not. The new engine, with its higher compression and reduced boost, produces a linear flow of power that totally does away with the explosive kick in the butt that used to characterize 911 Turbos. Thrust is immediate, effortless, and intoxicating at just about any speed. The PDK gearbox ($4550) has achieved a new threshold of refinement, shifting almost as smoothly as a conventional torque-converter automatic and responding instantly to manual downshifts and upshifts.

With the go-fast options—the PDK transmission and the Sport Chrono package ($3830), which includes dynamic engine mounts and launch control—Porsche says this new powertrain will fire the car to 60 mph in 3.2 seconds. But judging by our history of beating Porsche's performance claims, we expect the Turbo to hit 60 in 3.0 seconds or perhaps break into the twos.

We had no opportunity to objectively test the Turbo, but we did try the launch-control system. To engage it, you first press the "sport plus" button. Then you depress the brake with your left foot and floor the throttle with your right, illuminating a "launch control" light. When the brake is released, the system lights up the tires and manages the throttle and the clutch to make the best use of the car's prodigious four-wheel traction. The car leaves so hard that it induces mild vertigo.

While we had only the briefest shot at driving the new Turbo on a racetrack, the car did show great grip and vastly improved control at the limit. Our final judgment, however, awaits a longer track examination.

On the road in Portugal, the Turbo was a delight. Steering feel, as with that of all 911s, is excellent, with perfect weighting and great precision. The Turbo's ride is supple, though the real test will be how it feels on the much more pockmarked and noise-inducing concrete interstates of the U.S.

Overall engine noise is subdued at a cruise and stirring at high revs, now reaching to 7000 rpm, up from 6600. Unfortunately, the engine produced a pronounced resonance when we applied medium throttle while cruising at about 85 mph. It sounded almost like the classic four-cylinder boom of yesteryear and is out of place on this lavish Porsche.

The car is scheduled to go on sale in the U.S. this month, with a base price of $133,750 for the coupe and 11 grand more for the convertible. As usual, tens of thousands of dollars can be easily added to the price by checking too many of the endless options. Even so, the 911 Turbo delivers performance that competes with cars that cost substantially more, while providing everyday usability that most exotics simply can't match. In that regard, it retains the spirit of that original 1974 Turbo. ≡

THE NUMBERS

VEHICLE TYPE > rear-engine, 4-wheel-drive, 2+2-passenger, 2-door coupe
BASE PRICE > $133,750
ENGINE TYPE > twin-turbocharged and intercooled DOHC 24-valve flat-6, aluminum block and heads, direct fuel injection
DISPLACEMENT > 232 cu in, 3800cc
POWER (SAE NET) > 500 bhp @ 6000 rpm
TORQUE (SAE NET) > 479 or 516 lb-ft @ 2100 rpm
TRANSMISSIONS > 7-speed dual-clutch automated manual, 6-speed manual
DIMENSIONS:
WHEELBASE > 92.5 in LENGTH > 175.2 in
WIDTH > 72.9 in HEIGHT > 51.2 in
CURB WEIGHT > 3500-3550 lb
PERFORMANCE (C/D EST):
ZERO TO 60 MPH > 3.0-3.3 sec
STANDING ¼-MILE > 11.3-11.5 sec
TOP SPEED (DRAG LIMITED) > 194 mph
PROJECTED FUEL ECONOMY (C/D EST):
EPA CITY/HIGHWAY DRIVING > 16-17/24-25 mpg

COMPARO
No. 1

DOUBLE-DOUBLE
ANIMAL

WHICHEVER WAY YOU STACK THESE PATTIES, THE 638-HP CHEVY CORVETTE ZR1 AND THE NEW 500-HP PORSCHE 911 TURBO ARE WILD MACHINES.

by MARK GILLIES
photography by MARC URBANO

STYLE

37

Ever since the 911 hit U.S. showrooms in 1965, the Chevrolet Corvette and Porsche's most iconic car have been facing off on racetracks and canyon roads all over the world. And through the years, the cars have displayed immensely diverse characteristics: The American is straightforward yet effective and entertaining; the German is slightly strange yet undeniably sophisticated.

The layout of each car has hardly changed since inception. A 1965 Corvette used a fiberglass body and a transverse leaf spring out back. It looked cool but was a little low-rent inside, had a monster V-8 up front driving the rear wheels, and seated just two. It's the same with today's sixth-generation Corvette.

The output of that original Porsche 911—148 horsepower from 2.0 liters—was a bit wimpy compared with that of today's car (345 horses, 3.6 liters), but the horizontally opposed six still hung out behind the rear axle. The 911 has always had room for two full-size people up front and a couple of miniature versions behind them, as well as a

decent front trunk. And even those who could not care less about cars can see the family resemblance between that first 911 and its modern counterpart.

The first 911 with a turbocharger appeared stateside in 1976, powered by a 3.0-liter flat-six that made a relatively modest 247 horsepower and gave rise to the term "turbo lag." A combination of light-switch throttle response and scary lift-throttle oversteer, courtesy of the car's semi-trailing-arm rear suspension and all that weight out back, resulted in a car that intimidated even the bravest drivers on a wet road. Still, that first 911 Turbo was regarded as an out-

and-out supercar, a reputation it has held for the 34 intervening years.

That couldn't quite be said of the Corvette. Back in the early days of this rivalry, a Corvette would dole out a straight-line ass whupping to any 911, but by the time the Turbo arrived on the scene, the Corvette had been reduced to an emissions-emasculated shadow of its former self. Between the dawn of the 911 Turbo and the arrival of the 2001 Z06, the only Corvette that could be compared with the Turbo was the Lotus-engineered ZR1 of 1990 to 1995.

The Z06, based on the fifth-generation Corvette architecture, brought the car back into the supercar realm. The subsequent sixth-gen car was good enough to come in a close third to a second-place 911 Turbo in a three-car comparo in Germany ["The Sports-Car World Cup," September 2006], won by the Ferrari F430. So we eagerly anticipated putting the even faster, more

Racing's Most Famous Dry Lagoon

For one of America's most storied road courses, Laguna Seca, near Monterey in California, had humble beginnings. The land for the track was part of the Army's Fort Ord and was used as a firing range up to and during World War II. In the Fifties, the popular Pebble Beach Road Races ran through the Del Monte Forest near Carmel, but after Ernie McAfee was killed in his Ferrari in 1956, organizers—the Sports Car Racing Association of Monterey Peninsula (SCRAMP)—went looking for a new site.

They settled on an unused chunk of the coastal Army base and, with Uncle Sam's support, raised $1.5 million from local businessmen and built the paved track. The first race was held in November 1957. The track has been home to all sorts of major-league races since, including Can-Am, Trans-Am, Champ Car, and the American Le Mans Series.

The original track was 1.9 miles long, lengthened in 1988 to 2.238 miles with an infield loop to satisfy the organizers of world championship motorcycle races. In 2001, Mazda stepped forward as the official sponsor, and today the track is known as Mazda Raceway Laguna Seca. Busy most days of the week, it is used for a host of car and bike races, track days, corporate events, and also by the Skip Barber Racing School. –MG

38

FREE-RANGE BEEF

refined, and markedly more expensive Corvette ZR1 up against a 911 Turbo in early 2009. But when that time came, Porsche mysteriously couldn't find a car to make available to us for a comparison with a ZR1, a Lamborghini Murciélago, a Dodge Viper SRT10, and a Mercedes SL65 AMG Black Series ["*Un*natural Selection," March 2009]. The ZR1 won, and Porsche no doubt heard that the victory put Mercedes-Benz's aristocratic schnoz out of joint.

Since then, the Turbo, along with the rest of the 911 range that's based on the 997 architecture introduced in model year 2005, has been revised. This time, Porsche found us a Turbo, which we picked up in Los Angeles. Then, keys to a ZR1 in hand, we headed off to the great driving roads of central California and later to the Mazda Raceway Laguna Seca track.

2. CHEVROLET CORVETTE ZR1

This ultimate Corvette hides its bulging muscles under a relatively discreet set of duds. Only rabid Corvette geeks can tell at a glance; ZR1 clues involve its carbon-fiber roof, chin spoiler, and hood with a see-through panel. Look closer, and you'll see that forged aluminum wheels cover giant Brembo carbon-ceramic brakes that are 15.5 inches in diameter at the front axle, 15.0 inches in the back. Inside, the ZR1 has some subtle changes, but the overall ambience continues the low-rent tradition, especially compared with the dressy Porsche—certainly not what you'd expect in a sports car that stickers for $121,425.

Still, the big price buys a lot of performance equipment. The 638-hp, 6.2-liter supercharged V-8 LS9 engine features such niceties as titanium connecting rods and intake valves, a forged steel crankshaft, and a dry-sump oil system. The suspension has magnetorheological shocks that enabled Chevrolet engineers to use softer springs than in the conventionally damped Z06.

On narrow mountain roads, the Vette seems huge, although it doesn't feel all that big inside. The rear hatch, however, opens to an impressively sized luggage area. The minor controls may not look fabulous, but the ventilation, sound, and navigation systems are very intuitive, and the driving position and control layout are good. The seats suck, though: They don't have enough lateral support, and the backs flop around under hard acceleration and braking. It's details like this that make you realize that the base Corvette is built to a price (roughly $50,000), whereas the $158,085 911 Turbo is based on a car that starts at about $80,000.

Trolling highways at 80 mph or so, the ZR1 is surprisingly civilized, providing a supple ride with the adjustable shocks in "tour" mode. Wind, tire, and engine noise seems remarkably

CHEVROLET CORVETTE ZR1

THE HIGHS> *Stunning engine and exhaust audio, a hero at the track, amazing brakes, civilized everyday persona.*
THE LOWS> *You paid $120K and got that interior? Needs a steady hand on bumpy secondary roads.*
THE VERDICT> *A cudgel compared with the 911, but blunt instruments get results.*

The monster front brakes measure 15.5 inches in diameter. The ZR1 gets unique gauges, but the poor seats and the décor are shared with lesser Corvettes.

subdued at cruising speeds despite higher sound-level measurements than in the Porsche. In fact, the car's a bit disappointing in this environment unless the driver downshifts a couple of gears and floors the throttle, at which point the car simply disappears into the horizon, its V-8 emitting a strident growl.

When the ZR1 gets driven really hard, it livens up like a nerdy college kid who discovers beer and girls on spring break in Mexico. The engine note is a constant delight under heavy throttle, as is the way the car shortens the distance between corners. The steering, which is inert on-center, becomes livelier with cornering g-forces, and the Brembo brakes are sensational, even if the pedal is a bit soft. The shifter isn't the most willing on earth, but the engine has so much torque spread over so wide a band that shifting becomes almost superfluous.

On a bumpy back road, the Corvette is a bit spooky at first because the giant tires follow road contours a bit too closely and the horrendous horsepower overwhelms the best efforts of the stability system to keep the back end in check. It's possible to generate quite a lot of slip angle with the stability system engaged unless one sets it to a new wet-weather program that was introduced for 2010. In that instance, the system cuts power more quickly, in addition to applying the brakes, and the rear end steadfastly refuses to slide. It's odd to hear the engine misfiring as the throttle is mashed, but it's reassuring, too: With the system completely switched off, it's as easy to spin this thing in the wet as it is to lose self-control at an all-you-can-eat buffet.

The Corvette moves around a lot more than the 911. It dives more under braking, squats more under hard acceleration, and rolls more before it calms down in mid-corner, even with the shocks switched to "sport." Aside from that, it's blindingly fast over any stretch of blacktop and is a mighty

track weapon. On a cold day, the Vette lapped Mazda Raceway a full second faster than the 911. Down the front straightaway, our VBOX test gear recorded 130 mph for the Vette just after it crested a brow, where it went light and a touch sideways before settling down on the other side.

The ZR1 is still one of the most entertaining cars ever built. It's not for the faint of heart, but it's a visceral thrill that's worth setting every nerve in your body on edge. The car's a little rough around the edges but warmhearted underneath. It just wants you to have a good time, and it certainly delivers when you're in the mood. We're just glad that, in these perilous times, GM continues to make this car.

1. PORSCHE 911 TURBO
The Corvette was looking good. It was faster around Laguna Seca. It won the battle for grip on the skidpad (although the road-holding performance of both cars suffered

The Turbo's seats are as good as the Vette's are bad. The interior has a classy mix of leather, Alcantara, and aluminum accents. The steering wheel with proper paddles costs $490.

due to unfavorable track conditions). It stopped more dramatically. It's cheaper than the German. But it's not as quick in a straight line—and that was a shock.

The Turbo whistled from 0 to 60 mph in 2.9 seconds and from 0 to 100 in 6.8, 0.5 second and 0.8 second faster than the ZR1, respectively. At the finish of a quarter-mile, the ZR1's 128-mph trap speed was as good, but the Porsche got there 0.5 second quicker, at 11.0 seconds. Technical editor Aaron Robinson was wide-eyed over the way the Turbo launched, and he normally reserves that kind of reaction for rockets at Cape Canaveral.

The 911 Turbo simply got a whole lot better for 2010. Porsche started with the engine. The displacement is up from 3.6 to 3.8 liters, direct injection has been added, and changes were made to the turbocharging and exhaust systems. The result is 500 horsepower instead of 480 and 479 pound-

PORSCHE 911 TURBO

THE HIGHS> *Incredible off-the-line performance, communicative steering and brakes, very practical, easy to drive very fast.*
THE LOWS> *Disappointing engine note, gets even pricier when loaded with desirable options.*
THE VERDICT> *A roadgoing Tomahawk missile that lives up to your childhood-established expectations.*

feet of torque, up from 460. The $3830 Sport Chrono package, with which our car was fitted, has an overboost function that bumps boost from 11.6 psi to 14.5 psi and produces an additional 37 pound-feet (516 total) for up to 10 seconds at a time.

Also new to the Turbo is a beefed-up version of Porsche's twin-clutch PDK transmission (a $4550 option). It replaces the old Tiptronic five-speed torque-converter auto-

matic and is available for the first time with dedicated paddle shifters (an additional $490). The revised BorgWarner all-wheel-drive system now allows more rear-tire slip before appropriating additional torque to the front axle, to give it more of a rear-drive feel. To address complaints about too much understeer, Porsche fitted stiffer front and softer rear anti-roll bars, firmer and variable-rate rear springs, and recalibrated adjustable shocks. Plus, in an attempt to mimic a torque-vectoring rear differential, Porsche offers a $1320 option that gently brakes the inside rear wheel to reduce understeer: This insinuation phases out gradually above 75 mph and disappears altogether above 100 mph.

With all its dramatic strakes and scoops and beautiful 19-inch wheels, the Turbo looks like a 911 but with more malevolence. Inside, our test car came with the full catalog of Porsche options, even bright-yellow

LAPPING LAGUNA

MAZDA RACEWAY LAGUNA SECA
MONTEREY, CALIFORNIA
2.2 MILES

CORVETTE ZR1
1:36.8/81.8 MPH

911 TURBO
1:37.8/81.0 MPH

The 2.2-mile track offers a compelling blend of corners mixed with a 300-foot elevation change from the highest to the lowest points. The Corvette ZR1 was faster essentially because its better power-to-weight ratio enabled it to outdrag the Porsche along the front straightaway and up the hill between Turns 5 and 8. But the revised 911 Turbo is now a much better track car and is easier to drive fast than the ZR1.

At the men-from-boys Turn 9, both cars average 1.3 g through the left-hander.

Both hit 119 mph up the hill, but the ZR1's superior power-to-weight ratio puts it 0.5 second ahead.

The cars are equally matched here, averaging 73 mph through Turn 10.

Mashing organs to ribs: The 911 develops 1.5 g at peak braking. The ZR1 slows more gently, at 1.1 g.

The Corkscrew

Rahal Straight

Rainey Curve

Again, the 911 carries more speed through the apex: 77 mph versus 74 mph.

The 911 is planted, the ZR1 ready to rip it sideways, but they're neck and neck here.

Andretti Hairpin

The ZR1 explodes, hitting 121 mph by the finish line. The 911 hits 115 mph there but handles Turn 1's blind crest with more poise.

By midcorner, the 911 is going 49 mph compared with the ZR1's 45 mph.

Peak speed on the straight: ZR1, 130 mph; 911, 128 mph.

seatbelts ($540!) that raise the issue of taste in an otherwise supremely classy cabin.

Compared with the Vette, the Porsche feels more compact and wieldy even before the flat-six engine is cranked alive. The relationship between the seat and the steering wheel is exemplary. The car is also very practical for such a high performer, with a limited front trunk and more luggage space if the rear "seats" are folded down to form a shelf.

On the highway, the Turbo rides more stiffly than the Corvette, and its tires slap more over chewed-up pavement, but it's never uncomfortable. Putting the adjustable shocks in their "sport" setting is advisable only on a track, though, because it will rattle fillings loose on lousy pavement and buck the car off line over bumpy back roads.

Across country, the Turbo is, in the words of Robinson, "the android-controlled technobomb compared with the street-punk ZR1." The ease with which it's guided

at intergalactic speeds is just amazing. It turns into corners with alacrity and exits with the unruffled traction of all-wheel drive. The steering is weighted wonderfully and connected securely to the blacktop. The brake pedal offers otherworldly feedback, and the aluminum paddles click off shifts with a sniper's precision. The car is super-stable at jailbait speeds, and it covers most roads with the kind of fluency the Corvette can't match.

Our only slight disappointment involves the engine. The power band feels much narrower than the Vette's fat torque curve and the engine doesn't sound as good, either, with a muted wail under hard acceleration that's masked by turbo whoosh. A naturally aspirated 911 sounds far better.

At Mazda Raceway, the 911 Turbo wasn't as fast as the Vette, but it was much easier to drive hard. For most drivers, the greater tactility of the 911 makes it more enjoyable

because you don't need to be on the ragged edge to get gobs of feedback and driver involvement. At the limit, though, with the stability control off, a driver has to be judicious with the throttle because a big lift off the power can cause the rear end to swing wide. Keep the system engaged, however, and it's remarkably benign, even in the wet.

In the end, we say the Porsche is the better all-around car, showing the results of 34 years of uninterrupted honing and refinement, whereas the Corvette has finally begun to catch up after some years of neglect. The Vette also feels much cheaper than the $37K price disparity suggests. The fact that it came in second in this two-car fight may be irrelevant to some because we don't expect a Corvette ZR1 buyer to turn up at a Porsche showroom anytime soon, or vice versa. As different in character as their would-be owners, these lifelong rivals have never been more competitive.